Tact in Court

TACT IN COURT

SIXTH ENLARGED EDITION

CONTAINING

SKETCHES OF CASES WON BY ART, SKILL, COURAGE, AND ELOQUENCE

WITH

EXAMPLES OF TRIAL WORK BY THE BEST ADVOCATES, AND HINTS ON LAW SPEECHES

By JUDGE J. W. DONOVAN

AUTHOR OF

"*Skill in Trials,*" "*Modern Jury Trials,*" "*Speeches and Speechmaking,*" etc.

1915

LONDON

SWEET & MAXWELL, LTD , 3 CHANCERY LANE

| TORONTO
THE CARSWELL CO , LTD
19 DUNCAN STREET | SYDNEY, N S W .
LAW BOOK CO OF AUSTRALASIA, LTD
80 ELIZABETH STREET |

THE EASTERN PRESS, LIMITED,
LONDON AND READING

NOTE TO SIXTH EDITION

The continued demand for "Tact," beyond the double editions just closed out, calls for the issue, which is considerably enlarged, to contain some hints gained by four years' work on the bench, in a large City Circuit, where ingenious counsel contend with each other for success and victory—a school of practice more instructive than a law course; many hints being given as side-lights to trial lawyers, to which are added some lecture hints that come in the line of up-to-date lawyers

J W. D.

Detroit, 1898.

PREFACE

ADDISON says, the safest way to give advice is in the form of fables, and cites the case of Nathan to David as his authority. In this he shows that where instruction comes through story, incident, or illustration, it is better understood and more convincing. The writer aims to follow this line of advice where it is given. The advice given is mainly from others.

In "Modern Jury Trials," the first series of this kind of law books, issued in 1881, is given some forty condensed trials, with ninety pages of descriptive matter, forming a book of 700 pages. The size required a price beyond the reach of many, and yet it has sold by thousands, even going into Europe, and reaching the Third Revised Edition. The demand for it came from the older class of advocates, who preferred to read the great trials of the past and present in extended form.

"Trial Practice and Trial Lawyers" followed in 1883, and met with equal success in this country. It was confined mainly to descriptions of American Advocates, Preparing Cases for Trial, and the Conduct of Court Cases. Being about half the size of "Modern Jury" it was still found beyond the reach of very many young lawyers. The Bar demanded brevity.

Judging by the numerous letters received from advocates of national fame, like Matthews, Beach, Graham, Curtis, Dexter, Gordon, Davis, and their class, relating to these volumes, and a lack of similar mention by young men, it appears that something even more condensed and less expensive is still needed for the great mass of young lawyers, to meet which this smaller volume is issued.

Some of the articles and rules have already been quoted in several law journals and "Modern Jury," but are deemed worth repeating in this form by consent of publishers. Most of the Trial Rules are new, and have been gathered by personal visits to, and by letters from, able lawyers in nearly every city of the Union. This part of the book is especially instructive, as it contains the experience of hundreds.

The success of both previous volumes is due to the variety of talent that they naturally comprise in including so much of the art and skill of able advocates of their best, inspired by great events. Many of them have passed away, and the writer can speak with more freedom of their genius and greatness. From the greatest has come the warmest welcome and encouragement. Especially cheering were the generous words of the lamented Beach, who said in 1882, " How eagerly I would have read such books when I started in practice."

J W. D.

DETROIT *January*, 1885.

NOTE —This Fourth Revised Edition is larger by many pages than the three previous editions of this book, and embraces a part of Mr " Lincoln's First Murder Trial," with a case of " Self-Defence," and " A Teacher's Defence," " Nerve in Law," " Tact in Trials," &c., together with some additional Trial Rules and turning-points and part of a law lecture, believed to be of interest and importance to young lawyers.

J. W. D.

DETROIT *January*, 1889

INDEX

TACT IN COURT

---·‡·---

TO BE A LAWYER.

THE luxury of pleasing others, enjoyed alike by actors, singers, and lecturers, is shared by lawyers. They show it in looks, express it in words, and tell it in tones of speech that thrill and captivate hearers and inspire the young with an early desire to be like such leaders. With this longing after greatness few believe in the hindrance to success, and most young men allow a free fancy to picture the future in gilded colouring. As thought crosses leagues and spans oceans in space as soon and as easily as across the street, so the ambition leaps from youth to greatness without the steps that lead upward on the rounds of fame's steep ladder.

Very few people consider the step-by-step process required in reaching success in law practice. It will not come by accident. It may not come by years of earnest labour It will more likely come by tact and art, honesty and eloquence Actors reach their distinction by finding their forte and following it artfully, but they have a stage and play to enforce attention. Lawyers must wait like doctors for a first case, and, may be, for the first half hundred. To get

in the procession is a great advance for a young
lawyer   Once in the line, the rest depends upon
mettle, gift, accident, or industry.

To be a lawyer requires the skill of a stair-
builder, the art of an engineer, the eye of an artist, the
voice of an actor, and the genius of an experienced
machinist; it is more—it is to be all these in one.

The machinist has no more intricate work than
the master of a great trial.   The engineer needs no
more care nor the artist more shading to bring out
characters in the light of nature, nor does the actor
need more power to compel conviction than every
good lawyer should command.

In the light of this combination of quality is it a
marvel that men succeed only seldom in the legal
profession?   Is it not rather a high and noble calling
that demands such diversity of talents and such tire-
less energy in fitting the mind and body for so great
a part in life's business?

The lawyer of all men should know much of life,
and much of human nature.   He should be a novice
in nothing, and wide-minded in all things.   Not a
genius in everything, but ripe in broad knowledge and
general experience.   When he is this, if he fails, it
will be no fault of his own; and as Clay said of
the Presidency, that he had "rather be right than
President," one had better be fitted for a lawyer, and
never have the golden fame he desires, than have
ever so many trials and do his duty indifferently.

If I should give one rule of fitness, it would be
that innate feeling that you are born for the law;
and if after reading the record of other men's
struggles and triumphs you still feel undaunted and
courageous, and possess a voice and body and con-

stitution for such a life of study and perplexity, then adhere to your convictions like the old martyrs did to their religion, giving their whole life to the contest.

LAWYERS.

LAWYERS, the most trusted and distrusted · the men who make contracts and unmake them, who give advice and sell counsel, who make money out of trouble and make trouble out of money; who create estates and distribute them—legally; who live by loaning money, and often subsist on borrowed capital; who hear and conceal marriage secrets, and drag out faded letters in bitter divorces, who please and persuade when they are lucky, but often go out of Court branded and dispraised by the side defeated —and with one side always the loser what wonder that the slurs of character fall to the common lot of the lawyer!

Without the smiles of the merchant's customer, he meets the frowns of business men in trouble. No time is to be lost, no delay for fees. He must win a victory or bear the blame for ever Unlike the builder, who knows that, be it ever so perfect, the elaborate house he has finished can never suit the proprietor, unlike the machinist, he controls not his own enginery; carrying the double burden of care for self and client; invited to win what others have failed in, urged to mend the broken pieces of an ill-made contract; bound to account for unreasonable confessions, blunders, and letters; asked to replevin goods already secreted, to attach the effects of a malicious merchant, to unearth fraudulent elections, to reclaim vast estates from costly tax titles, to keep one for years in plenty by restored possession and broken wills, often on doubtful evidence, by a lawyer's art and eloquence—what a happy condition!

Fated from the start by uncertainty, where clients exact no less than absolute victory, they long to call reasonable what they know is only probable. By logic and argument on the theory of their client, with the facts only partially stated, and that part deeply shaded, they are often surprised by the other side and called to explain away their defeat in the end by a tirade on the perjury of witnesses and the depravity of human nature.

The happy lawyers! The men who live so easily, flourish so long on the bounty of a grateful people, make the laws and settle the titles, defend the weak and protect the wealthy, enjoy the rich fruit of the world's praises and abuses, mingled and commingled in such rare harmony that none can define where censure ends and approval commences! Who would not be a lawyer?

TRIAL PRACTICE: NOTE TO YOUNG LAWYERS.

"It is the mind that makes the body rich,"
—and the lawyer rich

A MAN's training for the Bar should include, besides a liberal education, six stories, seven legends, nine illustrations, and ten points of practice, with a voice to attract and convince hearers, as a starting outfit or capital for an advocate. With these at command, covered with poverty and its struggles to contend with, the prospects of a young lawyer are to-day very promising. It is observed, to begin with, that influence and riches are ignored as elements of success to a lawyer. These are no part of his training and a hindrance to his self-reliance, which is essential to a fitness for the high office of a good lawyer. He must stand alone and lean on nobody.

His office is opened. His case is on trial. He is the master and actor of the occasion. A rich father cannot help him win standing or character at the Bar —character is won alone.

What to say and how to say it has puzzled thousands and will puzzle more thousands to the end of time. The plain matter-of-fact speakers will rely on something to occur at the hearing. The more careful and experienced will save up a store of useful matter either of history, terse romance, pointed story, or touching incident, to fit in, finish, and embellish his reasons—forming thereby the drapery and finish or painting of the subject he has to describe. But over all he must *know* men! Our greater men are greater far than books; this book is made of *men*.

While Beecher was never able to quote either from hymns or poems, song or Scripture, he was never lacking in incident and apt illustrations. Webster, the heavy, and often prosy, was never at a loss for a climax to "raise mortals to the skies and drag the angels down"—a beautiful paraphrase of Dryden's saying

> " He raised a mortal to the skies,
>   She drew an angel down "

Crittenden was equally fetching with his legends of Man's Creation, where Truth, Justice, and Mercy are consulted. Truth and Justice say, Create him not; and Mercy prevails with her plea—"*Oh, create him, Father, and I will follow him, and by his errors shall he learn wisdom, and at last I will bring him to Thee.*" It is said that the effect of this legend in the Ward murder case was the most thrilling of all incidents at the trial.

The description by General Harrison of the first trial by jury in an open field, where the jury surrounds the coffin and the accused touches the wound of the victim, was the work of a master advocate in closing of Cold-Spring case, as was also the turning-point of General Brown's closing in the Hetfield trial, where the defence had dwelt on the broken family of the accused in case of conviction, and the ingenious counsel turned it by the apt words, that "mercy has another side to its picture; and before you go one way too far, go with me to yonder kirkyard, and, standing by the new-made grave of Calvin Hetfield, there witness the widow and three orphan children—made so by the hand of this defendant—and there between the living and the dead—*there in the presence of the ruin he has wrought—there write your verdict.*"

Can anyone doubt the power and influence of such sentences?—their fitness and controlling force? They are like apples of gold in pictures of silver to all hearers; and this leads to the gist of the topics in this volume, which are added as light on a lawyer's acquirements, with observations noted from the Bench during several years and over twenty years of trial practice, together with considerable reading on this subject, which has been and is the ambition of the writer's life.

The conclusion reached from observation and reading is—to be able to say a thing well one must learn it; to say it rightly he must have practice He will only gain information by intense reading and keen observation every day of every year, and will only show proficiency in presenting facts and reasons strongly after a thorough preparation. Life being short, at longest, it is urged as essential to success that one be diligent in business, and see to it that he has a storehouse filled with the rarest legends, most pointed stories, and most apt sayings of Bible, Shakespeare, and good authors, and plenty of touching illustrations to weave in. These, with a voice at command and wellspring of fitness, backed by character, will fill the exalted duties of an advocate. To make this beginning this book will help you, with its five hundred examples and illustrations culled from the best lawyers the world has ever known.

IN THE COURT ROOM.

Four years on Circuit Bench, with a single term in Probate and Recorder's Courts, confirms every rule laid down in " Tact " and emphasises many new facts in practice that may become useful.

1. Into the Court room sooner or later will come all phases and conditions of life and business—growing out of some lack of clearness of contracts, domestic quarrels, disputes over buildings and boundary lines, slander or libel, with the crimes that belong to the criminal cases.

2. No college or law school on earth can compare with the debates over these various cases as the facts

and law are directly seen in each instance and become impressed on the memory like a painting—the things we come in daily contact with and take part in are a part of our existence   This leads to the following observations or rules—namely :

(a) Lawyers waste too much time in talking; rely too much on it; tire a Court too often by it; repeat a story until it is threadbare and loses snap, pitch, or meaning.

(b) Lawyers in asking special verdicts of a jury by five questions—should so frame them that some at least will be rightly answered. The wrong reply is a double-edged sword.

(c) Requests to charge are nine times out of ten too numerous, and six times too long to be remembered. They are thus confusing and misleading to a jury. They create a hatred more than a liking for the counsel who framed them.

(d) As is repeatedly shown, to cross-examine a smart woman, boy, girl, or man is suicidal. It lets them get the laugh on counsel or the cry on the witness, and either is killing to the purpose. Why will young lawyers forget this? Why will they fool with edge-tools in darkness?

(e) A trained lawyer with TACT IN COURT will not be in on faulty pleadings. He will not be in on a breach of promise unable to prove a promise.

(f) He will not be in on negligence, unable to show his client looked and listened, or that he could have seen and avoided all that happened. He will show right of possession in Replevin and Trover, demand in both, and offer to turn back property in fraud cases.

, (g) A good lawyer will not bluster. No boxer, rider, racer, or ball-player even would start with a flourish; coolness proves ability, strength, and reserve power; it begets confidence; it is wisdom in Court practice.

(*h*) That your witnesses are candid is a strong lever. A silly, half-witted, half-captious " smart Aleck " is worse than no witness. Look out about being ridiculed It is a powerful weapon.

(*i*) More cases—ten to one—are lost than gained by trying to dig from the enemy what you should leave alone ("never wake a sleeping dog "), and rely on your own law and testimony.

(*j*) Disputing with the Court after adverse ruling is a weakness. It's idle and fruitless. It decides cases for the jury that they might decide otherwise, and yet fear to go contrary to the Court's ruling—once emphasised.

(*k*) Good lawyers know what they want and stop with it. Ask no questions that may be answered for the enemy. Leave what is done where a layman can notice it. Argue discrepancies with jury, and never with witnesses.

(*l*) Learn to rely on substantial, not trivial matters. Do the Lincoln act—catch the middle of cases and hold that part up like a painting to the Court or jury.

(*m*) Make the brief less wordy—more meaty and direct. Three good citations are worth ten poorer ones. Single-page briefs are always of interest.

(*n*) Know your law and facts before starting. Both sides ready? Yes, your Honour. But how often otherwise!

(o) Open clearly, tersely, candidly. Don't declare you will annihilate the enemy. You may not be so fortunate. Press a few points home with emphasis.

(*p*) Persuade and please by good methods. Anger rarely wins anything but applause from spectators. That is rebuked, and leaves you weak from the rebuke it invites.

(*q*) Question your parties carefully. A recent suit went to judgment when defendant was actually dead before it was started   An old firm-sign had misled the plaintiff. By all means, get the right parties.

(*r*) Rely on the right of matters. If you win and go wrong, of what use is it? If you deceive a Court on the law, a new trial will follow. If you get an unjust verdict, will it avail anything?

(*s*) Stand by your client, but take a fair position. He cannot ask you to clear him in all cases, if actually guilty. He will be pleased with a moderate sentence,—with a moderate verdict, with a fair adjustment.

(*t*) Think for yourself. Try every case as if it never should be tried again. Try it clearly, fairly, wisely, thoroughly—with your heart in your hand. "The hand is no stronger than the heart" in trial work.

(*u*) Rely on yourself in the Court room. The counsel will pick up but a part of the facts that took you days to learn from the witnesses. There is no counsel like the first one, with whom all facts are centred.

(*v*) Verify your pleadings by comparison. Study them after cooling time—an amendment may be given, if asked for. Be not too certain, or too hasty. Law is a science. Trial work is a science. Victory is a science. Wisdom is a science.

BOY DEBATERS.

As all trial lawyers must learn to argue and reason off-hand, in many cases, it is important that they learn to speak readily from habit—to think and compose while standing. Law life is not a railroad with resting stations; it is a quick line with few stops to take on baggage.

Young lawyers should join some debating-school quite early, and study the reason of things—should attend all good speaking, read books of human nature, study men, and, above all, have something to say. Save happy quotations, stories, and incidents, and be able to illustrate thoughts, so as to beget clearness, alertness, and convincing force in argument. Chauncey Depew invariably starts with a happy hit to gain attention, so does Colonel Irish, whose story is a crusher to an enemy. Desiring to show what could be done by a "scare," he told Joel Chandler Harris's story in the *Century*, like this: "It was at a coloured dance in South Carolina, under a pavilion, when a merry party was surprised by an animal better known than described. Seeing his approach, the ladies screamed and jumped on the benches; the men ran out, leaving the old fiddler alone with his visitor—when the animal spoke thus in fable· 'I ain't done nothin'. What do they run for?' The old fiddler leaned low and spoke: ' 'Tain't what you'se gone and done, Massa Skunk, cause yo' ain't done nothin' yet. *It's what you'se goin' to do. they run fur.'* "

By apt stories Lincoln won many cases. By their use Depew pleases people, and the art of pleasing is a wonderful acquirement for a Court room. No one will hunt stories for you; you must think for yourself. No one will look out for your opportunities; you must find them yourself. No one can help you half so much as yourself. You must be alert in training, up-to-date, and ready to do better than others   The difference between failure and success is industry and fitness.

The Golden Rule of all in practice, is to *be ready* with law and evidence. Make your own case by your own side's testimony. Stop when you get a ruling, make a point, or reach a climax. Let the other side kill their case by cross-examination if they care to, but leave such weapons to the unwary Act with firmness; hate no one; learn to please in persuading; rely upon fair jurors, clear testimony, and intense energy—with a thorough preparation.

GOOD LAWYERS.

A GOOD lawyer will have character, and by forecast reach results, if possible, before suit is brought, and if claim is sued will—

1. Select a jury with extreme care, rejecting jurors with a bias, interest, or of doubtful characters—one bad juror may hang up a panel.

2. He will not quarrel with a Court, but be so armed with ready proof and law as to convince the Court and jury of his claims. He wins who convinces.

3. He will open up his case with care and great clearness before evidence, and know that his facts may not be as clear to Court and jurors as to himself, as "All men are eloquent in what they know."

4. He will be frank, just, fair, and reasonable, and win by these methods and his clear proof and presentation of facts and circumstances. How many lawsuits are comprehended?

5. A good lawyer will be a gentleman, and not a loud-spoken boaster of what he can do. He will rather prove what he can do by doing it. Grant's *victories*, and not his reports of them, made him famous.

6. He will wire and 'phone freely, go to the scene of a failure, gather his facts at first hand, and be first, if possible, on the premises in replevins and attachments. Men pay best for superior skill in law matters.

7. He will possess the power to please and return pleasure, as success depends "upon the number he can make himself agreeable to." But nothing so pleases in business as a fitness and skill in one's chosen profession. These are his storehouses of fortune as a lawyer.

8. He will be alert, well-informed, friendly and convincing in manner, and withal a sincere man in business, by such means attracting clients and insuring confidence. This is the method of Choate, Edmunds, Carter, Harrison, and used by most excellent lawyers.

9. A good lawyer will of course be honest, keeping clients' money apart from his own, remitting promptly. and will be able by using his genius to serve his clients in emergencies; by counsel and Court work, will preserve their rights and estates as a sacred trust, as did Lincoln, Waite, Matthews, Porter, Seward, and Hendricks. Such lawyers and all leaders of the Bar have exemplified *integrity* in their lives as well as their practice.

CHARACTER AS CAPITAL.

IN direct contact with banks, merchants, and money men, where integrity is credit and skill is at a premium, the lawyer's rise in his profession depends upon his character.

Men who fail, as did Claflin, and even President McKinley, and later pay up their indebtedness, gain new character by the payments.

A lawyer whose personal standing is a fixture is like a golden eagle, and will win business through his integrity.

Commercial reports are based not alone upon property, but upon skill and success in the business that one follows. As life is short, says Goethe, one must choose early to do what he is best fitted for, in order to reap its rewards in season for enjoyment.

Character will place a lawyer with the company of good men. "To keep with the good, we soon become one of them," says the Spanish.

Relying on the acquaintance, skill, and integrity for his start in life, and using these as the tools of his profession, the tools must be kept in order and not rusty. It is for this reason that fresh books and new literature is an element to consider as a means of polishing up a rusty armour and enlarging one's line of acquaintance; by books we touch elbows and learn personally of each other; on wisdom we build character, with it we found friendship.

To-day it is the duty to bring back the child of a runaway wife whose partner in crime has abandoned the offspring To-morrow it is the handling of a fortune left one who heard of the lawyer's good deed just mentioned. Next day, it will be the trial of a suit before a Judge or jury who will in many ways give credit to character—so that every step up the ladder of fame depends in a large measure upon character. It is not enough to win lawsuits—some cunning counsel do that. It is not enough to be eloquent—some pettifoggers are convincing. It is not enough that one is a master of invective—very many can be sarcastic. The foundation of a lawyer's fortune is character—out of sight, yet never out of mind, and never out of hearing.

It carries Dillon to a New York City practice, it calls Curtis to San Francisco; it makes Edmunds a giant in higher counsels of law, and leaves the fame of Lincoln immortal as an honest lawyer.

Character grows from every transaction, little and large. To-day it is a small collection; next it is an intricate replevin or attachment; next it is a yearly salary for a half-dozen houses. It is built up from large and small cases. It is in attention to details; it is in integrity of remittance; it is in open and frank dealing; it is in the quality of the services and the fairness of your dealing.

HABIT AND CHARACTER.

LECTURE TO LAWYERS.

ALEXANDER the Great, on seeing the games that were attended by everybody, instead of looking on one day, became jealous of the players and said, "If princes only were my competitors I would enter the arena and run myself, for I have noticed" (rather gravely) "that all of the prizes and cheers are given to those who enter the arena and run, and none are given to those who stand looking on from the outer side."

So, whatever you do in life, you will be required sooner or late, in any position, to enter the arena and run; and the prizes of life, whatever they are, will not be given to those who stand looking on from the outer side, but to actual contestants in the arena. Let me make that still clearer by a figure:

Fernanz, in the way-back days, when things were told, not by writers and historians, but by legends— which, by the way are stories, and the fringes and the drapery and the finish and cornice of literature, because they are so old and so dainty that they bring before us a painting and a likeness of what they represent,—away back in the past, Fernanz was the genius of pleasure, and was believed to control the woods and groves, the streams and fountains, the sun, the moon, the stars, and even the destinies of young people. Having such power by the legend, he conceived the notion that training would have everything to do with the people—that in proportion as they were *trained* they would be elevated; so he selected a young girl, still in her mother's arms, too young yet to speak, and placed her in the charge of twelve maidens to be taught all the accomplishments of womanhood, and he directed her to be kept in parks and gardens, and entirely apart from the other sex, until she reached sixteen. He then selected a little boy, and placed him in charge of twelve philosophers and teachers, and bade them keep him separate from the other sex.

At the age of sixteen the young girl had grown up fair and beautiful, and in the park one day, passing by a fountain, she looked in and saw something in the water. She waved her hand and the hand waved in the fountain; she bowed and it bowed; she smiled and it returned the smile; and she said: "What is this I see? Ah, it is myself, it is the likeness of myself. Why am I so strangely formed? The woods, and the parks, and the flowers, all are beautiful that I may admire them and rest beneath their shade. But why, and for what purpose, am I so strangely made? Why am I so unlike the rest?" And growing sad and dreamy, she sat down by the side of a tree on the moss and dreamed. And in the dream she saw a being never seen before, and she sought to touch it, and reached out her hand to it to catch it, yet it eluded her grasp, till at last she awoke and saw right before her the young man trained by the twelve philosophers—a being she had never seen before. She shaded her eyes with her hand, and said: "Oh, this is a dream. This is my dream. Why did I not dream on? Why should I awake? Oh, what a beautiful dream!"

The young man approached her as though he were about to console her and talk to her, but he

had no words for such a person. He reached out
his hand as if to touch her hair. As he was about
to lay his hand upon her head, suddenly Fernanz
came forth and said: "Stay, withhold your hand.
Touch her not, but first learn this great lesson. It
is not her beauty that you see all at once" And to
the young woman he said, "It is not his manhood
you see all at once: it is the training of your life;
it is the training of his life, *it is the training of your
lives all the way up that has made you able to comprehend each other.* Now join hands and go through
the journey of life together, and so live that all the
world may know the use and strength and purity of
womanhood, and the power and wisdom of manhood."

Let it be made clearer by

A Story of Two Dogs.

Lycurgus said. "I would show thee, O king,
that a cultivated people must be a happy people."
But the king, thinking only of his dogs, paid little
attention to what the lawyer said; so the lawyer
tried him, as lawyers do, with a side-thrust, and said,
"I would show thee, O king, by the example of
my little dogs, that as the training is and as the
habit is, so one will be all through life."

On hearing the word "dogs," the king said,
"Bring in your dogs." Lycurgus brought in a pair
of little dogs, and he said: "I have here, O king,
my two little dogs—both the same age, having the
same mother. Now, this little dog on my left has
been trained in the house, and petted and fondled,
and fed on bread and milk; and this little dog on
my right has been taught to hunt the hare in the

woods for his master. Now, O king, I would have thee send for a platter of bread and milk and place it in the corner of the room, away from this little house-dog yonder, and I would have thee bring in a live hare and conceal it at the farther corner of the room yonder,"—which was done. "Now let go the dogs." And the little bread-and-milk dog made a leap across the room for the bread and milk and licked it up to the last drop, while the hunting dog started for the corner and ran round and round, and caught the hare and brought it to the feet of his master. And Lycurgus said: "You see, O king— you see by the example of these little dogs, that as the habit is and as the training is, so will one be all through life. So, O king, it is with men—so it is with men."

These are all bearing on the subject of habit. That will come right into your own life—right into your own calling. Take the German definition of success in life, "Mit dem Hut in der Hand, geht Man durch das ganze Land": that is, with the hat in the hand—with politeness—man succeeds in any country. Or take another sentence, which is just as deep, just as forceful· "Keep with the good, and you will be one of them; go with the bad, and you will soon be one of them." Or this, from Carlyle, just as good as either: "Success in life, *in anything* "— think of it, success in life, *in anything*—"depends upon the number of persons that one can make himself or herself agreeable to." If he is an agreeable teacher, he will have a large number of scholars. If he is an agreeable minister, he will have a large congregation. If he is an agreeable and capable

lawyer, he will have a large number of clients
If he is an agreeable and capable doctor, he will
have a large number of patients. If he is an agreeable
and capable merchant, he will have a large number
of customers.

I will bring the matter very directly to you by
the instance of a young man who helped me in my
business—make it personal, for he is now so far
away that he will not know about it. He is living
in Chicago, and very successful He came into my
office one day, and said, " I hear that a young man
lately in your office has gone away."—"Yes." " I
would like to have the chance to come in and take
care of your office, and serve your papers."—"But
you are a little too large, young man, for my price."
"How much is your price? "—"Well, I have only
been giving Martin three dollars a week." And
he answered, "I will help you for three dollars a
week, or you can fix any price " "Well, come in,
then, to-morrow. Is there anybody that you have
worked for here? "—"Yes, I have worked for
Colonel A——, General T——, and some others."
"How did you happen to leave the other places? "—
"Well, I wanted to go where there is a smaller
business, where there is a kind of business I can
learn. They have all large cases, and I want to go
where I can learn the whole business better."—"Very
well, come in." He came in, and behaved himself
very nicely, and stayed seven years, and then found
that he took to railroad law. He wanted to go to
a large city and do railroad and commercial work,
and auditor's work. It seemed to be the special
work that he was inclined to.

He took a letter which he presented to the Illinois Steel Company. The letter said, " I feel like giving him a good name, which is worth more than a thousand dollars." He presented the letter to the manager, who read it, and seeing that part about the good name worth more than a thousand dollars, said, " I like that—a good name is worth more than a thousand dollars." How long have you been with him? "—" Seven years."

The Illinois Steel Company was a fourteen-million dollar company, and he was made second auditor. He settled claims all the way from Springfield to Wisconsin, and did a large business. A few years ago, he started on his own account, and has settled a great many cases since then.

Did he deserve the position? Let me read a letter that they gave him, after being there a year. The letter read like this:

" Mr J. B M. ——City.

" Dear Sir,—Find enclosed our cheque for Five Hundred Dollars, apart from your regular Two Hundred Dollars per month salary, which we trust you will accept as a slight reminder of our good wishes in your behalf

" Signed,
—— Sec'y, Steel Co "

What an elegant letter! Especially the cheque. Do you know what I mean when I say that I have, for each of you, a fortune on conditions? And what are the conditions? The conditions are that you will be ready to accept the fortune, and there will be no mistake about it, and so that the fortune will not be misspent. I will make that a little clearer.

I took a young man over recently to one of the largest concerns here in the city, to the Majestic Building, and introduced him to the head of the house, and directly the head of the house commenced to cross-examine him in this way: "Have you ever had any experience in the clothing business? "—"No, sir." "Where have you been? What have you been doing? "—"I have been with Glenn & Hunter." "What did you do there? "—"I worked on the elevator." "How long were you on the elevator? "— "Not long." "Then what did you do? "—"I sold books and other goods about the house." "How did you happen to leave there?" (note the cross-examination). "Why do you want to come in here? "—"Why, I want to learn the clothing business." "Well, what kind of a position do you expect to get in the clothing business, and how much do you expect to get? "—And the answer was: "I want to learn the business. I want to find out if I can come in here and learn the business. I did not come to fix a price, I came to learn the business." "Well, young man," patting him on the shoulder, "I like that, I like the way you talk about it. Come in on Monday. Come in at eight o'clock. Leave your name at the third floor at the desk. We will see how you get along."

Very recently I walked up Michigan Avenue with the man that had cross-examined him, and I asked him how the young man was getting on. "Splendidly He wore out a good many vests for us in piling up stock, but he is getting along all right, and is now a salesman. He is getting along splendidly I like him, and I am very glad you brought him in; he is a good boy."

This is one of the fortunes, and this is one of the conditions that I have brought to you that you must fulfil, in order to gain the fortune. You must be ready. Are you ready? I doubt it. You may think you are ready, but let us see. What can you do now? Can you add a column in a bank ledger so that you will know that there is no mistake? I doubt it. Can you add it up so that you are willing to say that if there is any mistake you would be willing to make it up out of your own pocket; that in adding up that whole column of figures of that ledger you would be ready to say, when you put down the figures, that they are just the same as dollars to you, and if there is a mistake made in any of them it would be dollars to you, or dollars out of your pocket? Are you ready to do that? Are you ready to go into a store and meet people? Can you do it? The power to please, the power to return pleasure in life, depends upon the number of people you can please. Are you ready to do that? You are being trained here, you are going step by step like the girl in the park, like the boy in the park—you are being trained. Are you ready? Not quite yet. Lincoln said, after he had studied surveying eight months, that he had so mastered it that he was willing to fix the line of a farm and abide by it, if it were his own farm. He was willing to fix the corner of land and abide by it, even if it were his own land Accuracy, complete accuracy, mixed with politeness and the power to please, is something you must learn and remember.

These fortunes that I have brought to you, and that I give to you, will not apply to each one

exactly the same : to the young boy it will be one
thing, and to the young man it will be another, but
"the hat in hand," the success in life, the power to
please men, applies to all.

Matthew Arnold said that most of us are what
we must be, not what we should be, not even what
we know we ought to be Most of us are what we
must be by circumstance and by habit, not what
we should be, and not even what we *know* we ought
to be. I promised to say something in this connection
about habit and about character, because they have
all to do—habit and character have all to do—
with each other. Let me bring in one figure here
and illustrate this.

You remember three or four Sundays ago, on
Woodward Avenue, a great line of march went
down, headed by a brass band, followed by the
military companies of the city; they followed by
the G. A R , and the G A R followed by the
Union Lodge, and the Union Lodge followed by
the Damascus Commandery, and the Detroit Commandery followed by a hearse, and in that hearse
a body, and back of the hearse *a riderless horse*,
draped in black, and all this vast procession coming
down Woodward Avenue one Sunday afternoon, a
mile long, in honour of General Robinson. And
why did so many lodges and men turn out, and so
many bands, and so many soldiers, and so many
people turn out for him who would not turn out for
another person?

This is why · General Robinson had a character
in the community; he had a character in the State,
he had a character in the nation How? Simple
enough. He had a local character in the community

in which he lived; he was a surveyor, a good business man and upright citizen. But his great national character was gained by one single act. The Sir Knights were down in Baltimore. The Detroit Commandery, headed by Eugene Robinson, were on march. The Knights of the whole country were there in competition at Baltimore. This was about the early seventies, and across the streets were old-fashioned stepping-stones, where the water could run between, and a person could walk over the crossings.

On the day of the march a tremendous rain-storm came up, and the word went out "It rains, and we will not go out to march." But Eugene Robinson looked over his company and said, "WE GO OUT, sure enough!" and the word came to the hotels, and the street windows were all crowded with people to see the march. The rain poured down on the white feathers of their hats, and every step their feet sank in the mud over their blackened shoes. Yet on they marched, while the rain came down in torrents as the turn of the Detroit Commandery came to make its manœuvres in the main street. Like clockwork, like an architect's scale, was the plan laid out—twenty-seven inches for every step, so many steps for a square, and every star and cross, so many companies front, and so many battalions front. They went through the long manœuvre in the rain, and passed the Carelton House All eyes were looking on the Detroit Commandery Every company in the line had swung out from the main line and walked on the stepping-stones, but Eugene Robinson had a better command than that, and, marching step by step, his knights

3

went splash, splash, straight through the mud, never
turning to the right or to the left, and General
Robinson touched his feathered hat as they went
through and said, "That is right, boys on duty
turn neither to the right nor to the left, but go
forward."

And the word went all over the nation, and the
Detroit Commandery secured the banner. On duty,
young man and young woman—on *duty*, turn neither
to the right nor to the left, but forward, always
forward. That is the fortune that makes fame, that
is the habit, that is the training, and that was the
training of Eugene Robinson

I have asked you what you could do, and there
is one thing I wish you to remember. Habit will
have everything to do with your life when you enter
into business Take, for instance, the case of a
young man I had with me, whose name I will not
call. We were together a good many years, and
there was a habit in the office, when anybody would
come in, to say, "Well, John, what can we do to
make you happy?" Now that is a very simple
and careless sort of an expression—"What can I
do to make you happy?" Frequently this young
boy would say the same thing · "Well, Mr Clee,
what can we do to make you happy?" Now, as I
say, that is a very simple thing, but it has a great
deal to do with happiness after all. Happiness is
something that you can hand over to somebody else
just as readily as you can misery It is just a
matter of habit. For instance, we have a few
lawyers here in the city that hate everybody—and
nearly everybody hates them. And we have a few
lawyers in the city—your own lawyer here is one—

that have a habit of liking people, and they make everybody else like them.

Let's see; I wish to give you the fortune of happiness, and I wish to fix it in your minds and write it on your brain, so that you will have it The whole secret of it is this—and if I have not said another thing here to-day that you can carry away with you, let me ask you to remember this one little thing, and it will be a fortune worth having. What is happiness? What is this happiness that you are seeking? The Greeks sent out their Seven Wise Men to find the secret of happiness, and when they came back and said. "We have to report, a healthy body first, a moderate income next, and a well-stored mind last these are the elements of happiness,"—the people, a little wiser than anyone, said, "What about friendship?" The old wise Greeks went back again to their study, and came out and, bowing very low, said, "We have to report, a healthy body first, a moderate income next, a well-stored mind third, and a suitable number of well-selected friends last · these are the elements of happiness, and all the elements of happiness "

This is one of the fortunes that I have brought to you You must see to it in every position in life that you have healthy bodies; see to it that you stand erect, that you stand like men, that you build yourselves, that you have heels, that you have feet, that you have arms, that you have eyes, that you have bodies, and that you can use them. They are yours, and they are wonderful gifts. Think of it. Think of the blessing and the power and the fortune that you have, and think of it so that you

can use it; and see that you have the stored mind
and good habits that will bring you friendship and
will bring you success. Let me make that a little
plainer.

A real good man went over the plains with me
to Mexico—a man that I have eaten many a good
dinner with in New York and Chicago, and we
have spent many a day happily together—a man
from whom I have drawn large fees; and this man
lost his position, and he told me afterwards how
he lost it. I went to New Mexico with him, for a
house in New York, to close out a post-trader's
store. I came back and he gave me eighteen
hundred dollars to put in the People's Savings Bank,
and he remained in New Mexico. In a little while
he commenced to write letters to the house—long
fault-finding letters, and quarrelsome letters; and
the house one day sent him a letter back (they had
been paying him $2 500 before): they said, " Seeing
we are unable to agree together, we will discontinue
our store in Fort Stanton, and your services will
not be needed after the 1st of May." Services will
not be needed after the 1st of May! Oh, what a
crusher! Poor man! Many a day since then he
has been working at a stipend of fifteen dollars per
month. Why? He offended the house by saying
too many contrary things to them. Instead of
pleasing them, he displeased them, and they had no
use for him.

Take an instance here in the State of Ohio, where
I was born. A farmer had a very large farm, and
the railroad tried to cross it, and he fought the
railroad to prevent it from taking his farm. He
did not like to have his farm crossed by the road

in that manner. He thought it would spoil his
land. He fought it year after year in Court, and
at last the railroad won, condemned his land, and
built the road. His anger, that he had nursed for
years, got the better of him. He took rails and
threw them on the track, and along came a train
and jumped the track and killed two persons.
The man was arrested, tried, convicted, and im-
prisoned, and has been for thirty-seven years in the
penitentiary in the State of Ohio! While he has
been in the penitentiary all these years the land has
been improving, and a city has grown up on the land,
and the railroad which had run on his farm runs
on, and the man is a millionaire. His family has
made a million dollars by the city growing up in
the place where it would not have grown but for
the crossing of the railroad, and he is walking up
and down a narrow cell mourning for his liberty—
lost by hatred.

I bring this out to show the background and the
darkness—to show something that would hinder you
from the fortune, as it hindered him. It would hinder
you from happiness, as it has hindered him, and as
it hinders him to-day. That is, anger. Instead of
the power to please and to return pleasure, he had the
habit of hatred and anger.

But I find my time is almost up. I wish I had
another hour, but I must come to the end as soon
as possible.

There was in 1852 born in Russia a little child,
so strangely deformed, so awfully deformed, that
the mother wished it would die. Where the head
of the child should be was the twisted form of a
hand, cramped up on the forehead as if to deform

it unmercifully; and where the right hand of the child should have been was the rounded, bulky head of a child. Of course the thinking part was in the right place, but here was the right hand, in the forehead. The parents wished that the little fellow might die. It would be a mercy, so they said. But he did not die: he lived, and grew, and with his little bright twinkling eyes in the deformed head. The child became a man—an author, a writer, a poet, a leader of men—*Prince Trapolkine*.

But think of the difficulty that he overcame with his twisted head—the hand of the child where the head should be—and yet overcoming it all and becoming great. You can overcome anything. You have a fortune; but there are conditions: *you must think for yourself*, you must plan for yourself, you must be upright for yourself, you must use that body for yourself, *you must train yourself*, you must be ready to enter the arena for yourself and run, no one else can do it for you.

Let me say one word more in closing (for I have just a little more time) on this subject, and that is this. Write it on your heart that of all things, if you would succeed in life, the one thing that you must have is integrity—manhood You must have integrity of character. I find the best example in the Bible. You will find it in the book of Job. Job was the man who had lost everything—lost his flocks and herds and his fortune, lost his relatives and lost his health, and as he was out in the yard with ashes on his head and sores on his body (for he had endured privations, pain, and sorrow) even his own wife came to him and said, "Job, isn't it about time now to curse your God and die?" And then

he seemed to rise up like a new man, and you can
almost hear him as he stood up and said· "You
talk like a foolish woman Shall we receive *good*
and not *evil* at the hands of the Lord?"⹁ No, no,
and here is the wise saying "*So long as the breath
remains in my body, mine integrity shall not depart
from me.*"

BEACH'S START IN LAW.

THE death of Wm. A. Beach, "the noblest Roman
of them all" in advocacy for the last decade, recalls
his start in law practice.

His father was a well-to-do tradesman in Saratoga,
New York, and gave William a good education in
the academy near home, and his admission to the Bar
was considerably later; for the old gentleman had
peculiar notions of how "Gus"—that was his boy's
name—should pursue his studies.

After spending something over a thousand dollars
on the young man's education, he questioned him
of his future plans and prospects—of what he
wanted to do for a living. The young graduate
had not the faintest notion of law at that age, and
replied that he did not know. "I want you to
be a lawyer," said the father decidedly. The young
man hung his head, and replied, "How can I get a
library?"

He was an early lover of books and fishing, and
kept up both for a lifetime. "I'll hire you," said the
father, "if you'll work faithfully and obey orders for
the first year or so, and you will have a stated salary
and enough to buy books when the time comes."

"I'll do it," said William; and accordingly he was furnished with a Bible, a copy of Shakespeare, and Bunyan's "Pilgrim's Progress," and sent to live with a farmer uncle in the mountains, some twenty miles away. It was some days and weeks before he became interested in the Bible (each book was to be read three times thoroughly and notes made of it); but the young man became interested, fascinated, and charmed by each volume. He mastered them, and received with this victory a splendid vocabulary.

He was still diffident, and when he commenced practice he was timid and ungraceful. Still *he had ideas* in his language, quaint illustration, strong sentences, little words and clearness of putting things. The boys would say, "Let's go down and hear *Gus Beach* plead a case," and would go out of curiosity; but they would turn away, charmed by the little things he had said, and later they would change the saying to, "Let's go and hear YOUNG BEACH speak" And so, by degrees, he grew to be a fine reasoner, an attractive speaker, and late in life had a charm about all his speeches that was almost irresistible. Socially he was genial and affectionate. About five feet ten, and one hundred and sixty pounds weight, with a face and voice and manner not unlike Beecher's, an erect carriage, acquired in the military academy, I saw him personally in 1882, and liked him at sight. I heard him at his best in '73, when he could thrill me as no man before had ever done Everything about his tone, manner, words, and expression said: "Come nearer; throw off all surface dignity. *I am a man,* as well as an advocate."

POWER OF ILLUSTRATION.

ILLUSTRATION is using one familiar fact to show another newer fact in question. The familiar one is presumed to be beyond question.

The ancients were ever alert to enforce a point by illustration. A father, to shew his son the evil effect of excessive drink, would have an intoxicated slave brought in, and ridiculed in the presence of his children. Fables and short sayings, facts drawn from example, were favourite means of making strong reasons impressive.

It is perhaps the more usual method of argument employed by the great mass of people, and hence the more taking before juries and audiences, and for this reason matters are still reasoned out by comparison. There is a certainty of conviction to all such arguments. They come like the sound of a triangle in a band. They please many senses at once. They capture the ear, interest the mind, and hold the attention, while all along the judgment is active to detect the slightest lack of analogy.

He who reasons by story or incident must reason accurately, or he plans certain defeat. It will only be effective if made lucid and applicable, never when abstruse and uncertain. A rare fable, a short pithy story, or a forcible Bible quotation will take with a crowd, or jury, and create sentiment.

Daniel S. Dickerson and Chauncey Shaffer, both in their days able New York lawyers—the last still in active practice, the first long gone to his last reward—were each great rivals in the use of apt Scripture. Mr. Shaffer had the faculty in a rare degree of aptly using terse comparisons. "Evidently," he would say, "this is like the old fable of the lion and the fox, where the fox is shewn in the picture to be leading the lion, and a stranger remarks · 'Surely that picture was made by a friend of the fox! Had the lion's friend made it, it would show the lion as leading!'" So he applied the fable to the shading of the testimony by interested witnesses.

But of all men who convinced others by story none exceeded the lamented Lincoln, who was complete master of the science. Born in humble life, and gaining his wisdom largely by experience, he relied on the homely expressions of daily intercourse with the people. He was an adept in frankness of expressions. His stories used in reasoning seemed so plain that they were heard as in italics. They were perfect climaxes of logic

There is one other reason why illustrations convince men. They take everyone off guard; they come to the senses like a song, and songs are often convincing. They are delivered in a pleasing natural tone, and that is convincing. No one tells a story in any but a conversational key, and if that tone once catches the ear at all it is attractive. Senator Morton employed this method, and could hold a ten thousand audience two hours and over, speaking in a low tone while sitting in a wheel chair

I think that it is safe to conclude with Governor Wisner's reason in an arson case. In shewing why the straw-stack was not burned by combustion in mid-winter, he said· "It may be, gentlemen, I believe in the Almighty's power to do it, but I never knew of His walking twice around a straw-stack to find a dry place to fire it, with double-nailed boots on, so *exactly* fitting the ones worn by this defendant."

TACT IN TRIALS.

An advocate of eminence who was long noted for his many trial victories in criminal and fraud cases, very lately gave me two rules of practice that he considered important to remember. For clearness before a jury and courtesy to a Court they are models worth saving.

"I have observed," he began, "that lawyers almost invariably talk over the jury, and reason, like Senators and Congressmen, with big long sentences; while juries reason like women, with one or two simple examples like this: ' If one man failed to meet his note when due and cheated some one, they knew another of the same class of business would certainly be likely to be just as dishonest.'

"I found farmers had one language, carpenters had another, country merchants had another, and labourers another—these are the average jurymen. I adopted and used their catchwords and phrases, not as a 'clap-trap,' or a 'trick,' but 'to talk in their own language.' I found it took better; they understood me and knew my meaning better. I never lost my suit by a jury's ignorance of what I contended for.

"Another rule was this: Juries respect with unbounded confidence the leanings of a Judge. There is a reverence, that is often too exalted, but it is real. This was my experience, and I fell in with it.

I found it useless to argue after a ruling. I fell in
with the views of the Court all I could. I will give
this instance:

"At a trial of importance before Judge L., just
before adjournment one evening, he said, 'I may as
well announce to counsel that I will rule so-and-so
as to the law of this case.' This was fatal to my
position, but I bowed to the Court pleasantly and
said, 'That relieves us of dwelling upon that part,
your Honour,' and we went home.

"Opposing counsel argued very tamely on his
facts, and relied upon his victory in the ruling,
and I followed, prefacing with the remark that
our duty was much lessened, and I felt pleased at
it and at the candour with which the learned
Judge had shortened the controversy, to which
ruling I made no objection. But the leading issue,
I urged—the great vital, pivotal point, and the
merit of the issue, the Court must leave to the
solid sense of the twelve men before me—men not
so learned in the law, but far broader and more
experienced in affairs and dealings of man with
man, than either lawyers or Courts could ever be
expected to become, for a jury of lawyers could
never agree. The Courts of the several States were
often in conflict, but common sense and the jury
were one! In this manner I separated the jury's
duty from that of the Court and won a splendid
verdict, *over an adverse charge*, by *not appearing to
be hurt by it*—a verdict that was quickly followed by
a just settlement"

If these instances are not clear and instructive, I
will not render them less so by any attempt at pointing
out their moral.

TOO MANY COUNSEL.

WILLIAM H. SEWARD believed in the power of one counsel over many. He relied more on his own resources than any American advocate. "If you employ counsel, they will match you," was his advice to clients.

It is a common boast of many litigants that they have employed "General Bradley," "Colonel Carlisle," or some high-sounding titled orator, as if that alone were a fore-ordained victory. Trusting to this method is like leaning on a broken reed. Great counsel may give wisdom and dignity to a defence or prosecution, but they do not *create evidence*. Besides, if they are numerous, neither one will burn the oil in looking up law or search the town for evidence to sustain a theory. Indeed, there will be often a lack of harmony in theories with too many counsel.

Divided responsibility is one way to unsettle the true way of winning a verdict. The Union army never won so many victories as it did after Lincoln passed the sole command under Grant, and told him to go ahead and put down the Rebellion. I remember a recent instance where on one theory certain victory must have followed. It was a plan of the attorney of record. He had dreamed it out and mastered its details But the senior counsel distrusted its efficiency, took a different course, failed to do with the law what his associate had planned to accomplish with evidence, and lost. "That Judge has ruled squarely against the law," said the senior. But this was no great encouragement.   The junior knew the Judge was over-prejudiced.   To match this he had prepared a flank movement, which was abandoned in deference to *wiser* counsel.

The responsibility of a direct plan, and evidence to match—an early theory consistent with reason and common-sense—should belong to a limited number, if more than one.   The counsel that first surveys the ground, converses with witnesses, takes in the early situation, should control the trial   Absolute certainty in evidence is the best means of success.   The law portion need never be ignored, but the case will turn on other than law questions fifteen times out of twenty.

A COMMON-SENSE RULE.

COMMON-SENSE is a taking quality in reason and argument.   There is no better definition to trial logic than the truth so clearly told as to convince hearers.   If it is over-told, argued too much, it may shew anxiety, while a clear statement is taking and attractive.

Many witnesses testify under a strained belief that they must make a strong shewing, and counsel take the same course by over-argument.   If thirty men should swear they saw a man leap over a tall building, and only one should deny it, by shewing how he jumped from an upper window, the one would win over the thirty.

We may as well take it for granted that Court and jury have common-sense, and believe that facts must have a foundation.   The very moment one reasons from a longing to say something, he is losing, and truth from a witness will be of double force if told without shading.

The first step in reasoning is to secure attention. This is to be done by calling to mind some few points on which no one can possibly question your position. Garfield captured a convention by telling of a storm at sea

Having this goodwill of the jury, you are in the same position as one who has paid several notes in bank at maturity; it creates confidence, and, more than that, if tersely told it raises expectations and meets them. It is like telling a good story—the next story will be heard with new interest.

Stories are good to use as second kindling-wood, but dangerous to start with. The jury will not be ready to laugh or cry too early in the contest: save them for the supreme moment. Let the best argument come in unaware. You need not ring a bell or blow a horn to announce it; let it reach the better judgment of the jury at the right moment. when feelings are warm and receptive.

Appeals to sympathy are used effectively when they come by surprise, and grow, as it were, out of the characters in the controversy—anything that happened in the hearing of the jury, if apt, is excellent. There are topics that carry a jury and Court in a climax of victory by their simple recital. the jury will take credit for discovery. It may be the very argument they would make, and they will be proud of its application.

It is not often that a jury can be reached from the front in battle, and a flank movement may be better. A Western counsel made an appeal for the

release of a young boy, charged with arson—a
terrible offence, not clearly proven—by this side
illustration: "To a boy like this, life is little thought
of, and punishment is hardly realised. He sits here
as cold as marble. Brought in unironed and on
bail, surrounded by some friends who love him, he
has not yet learned to realise the consequences of
an adverse verdict. The chief anxiety is to the older
members of his family. To them his conviction would
be worse than the grave. When the little Farrington
boy was crushed to death the other day between
two huge trucks, and Dr. Eddy folded his broken
body in his fatherly arms and carried it home, the
scene was one long to be remembered. But the
parting of a mother with a convict son—to know
that he is to linger in his youth ten or a dozen
years in anguish—is a far deeper sorrow. Sooner
or later all home relations will be severed. Death,
with noiseless footfall, comes in, 'seals up the
doors of breath, puts out the light of the eye,
freezes the purple current of the veins, and we lay
them to rest for ever, and go away in sadness, for
a time,' but even *death is not* dishonour! It is not
like consigning one to a living tomb—not so dreadful, not so terrible in its consequences; and *of all
things to a jury, the first and middle and last
consideration is the* CONSEQUENCES OF THEIR VERDICT."

THE JURY

A GOOD jury, a good theory, and a sensible conduct in trials is a golden Court rule.

In addressing any large body of men, only a few faces will attract the speaker's attention, and these will be generally the middle-aged or the younger classes. Their keen eyes and expressive faces will show an early interest in every apt illustration or happy turn in the argument They see a point readily and comprehend its meaning. If they have not been bored by tedious discourses, or soured by disappointments themselves, they are ready to reason with the speaker and come to his conclusion when sensible.

But suppose they are withered up, crusty, conceited, or biased men, like ex-officers, who have been led to believe in the total depravity of mankind generally, and men engaged in lawsuits in particular. then you are on the losing side before your case is even started. What could have been gained by strict attention is lost in prejudice What should have come to your rescue in the form of candid willingness to listen is transformed into a lot of blocks and stones to hear your urgent appeals for justice or convincing logic on questions of evidence.

The young men who hear readily and appreciate the fact that generous natures may be misled, and even err unintentionally, should not be set aside for colder natures who harden their hearts habitually and are destitute of all charity. Reasoning men well know that 76 per cent. of real criminals are born into crime, and only 24 per cent. are accidental and occasional law-breakers. Accident, anger, insult, or bad company may lead to arrest when the defendant is either innocent, or never likely to become a criminal And as Governor Seymour once well said, " They may be the stronger for it than some who have never been tempted " This reasoning will only apply to fair-minded, warm-blooded, noble-hearted men. So that the audience—or jury—is of vital consequences in all cases.

To have an intelligent theory, and one founded on reasonable circumstances, is next in importance to a well-selected jury. It is too late after the witnesses are sworn and the jury is selected to form theories to match them; theories should be matured and managed like the artful turn in the great Barnard burning case, where a dying declaration of how a murder was committed became utterly worthless when the defence proved the one making it was in the habit of waking suddenly from vivid dreams, and relating most minutely every fact and circumstance of the dream like a living reality.

To conceal these theories from the enemy, and impress witnesses to do likewise, is excellent general-ship. This is never accomplished without the greatest caution. It is the natural bent of clients to boast of expected victories, and by it they only double their enemy's energy. Could they but surrender cases candidly to their counsel, as a patient places his life in the hands of his physician, many a case lost would be easily won, while the management would be freer from errors and blunders.

The anxious suitor is a thorn in the side of his counsel, and, like the spur of the race-rider, makes a break in places where evenness is of all things desirable. "Ask him this question." "Ask him that question." And to each a bad answer comes back, and the case grows worse by the left-handed manner of interference. The client is actuated by anger, and forgets that when a witness starts to tell a falsehood he will increase its clearness at every round.

There is little to be gained, and much to be lost, by meddling About all that can be gained beforehand is the full strength, and not the weakness, of the enemy, while clients constantly underrate their opponent's evidence, they would be wiser to magnify it, and be ready to explain or answer it with consistent honesty. Instead of placing stress upon character evidence, which of all things is dangerous—unless the character is beyond question, and the quality of witnesses to sustain it is equally reliable—one had better make the case without it, for any juryman will naturally reason that a doubtful associate would alone create a suspicion on a good character, while virtue need not boast too much of virtue.

The character of witnesses may often destroy the case they are sworn to sustain. I remember a breach of promise case where all went on swimmingly for the defence until a vile creature, called a man, swore to such a preposterous story of the plaintiff's acts with himself that not even a cross-examination was offered to deny it. It was considered its own denial, as it stood so revolting to reason that the common-sense of the jury rejected it and gave the plaintiff $10,000 damages.

If anyone believes that a foolish jury, or a stubborn jury, or a biased jury, or any but a fair-minded and intelligent warm-hearted jury, is the right one to try a civil or criminal case before, he lacks experience. If he believes in deceitful practices he is unworthy the name of *lawyer*.

THE JUROR'S OATH.

THE following opening period by Israel Holmes was originally intended to appear in " Trial Practice," but reached the author too late for insertion. It is a gem, and is given a place here

" Very beautiful and impressive is the juror's oath · *I do solemnly swear, that I will a true verdict render, according to the law and evidence, so help me God!* In the thousands and millions of times that this oath has been taken it has lost none of its beauty and none of its impressiveness. To him that rightfully takes it, whether believer or unbeliever, Christian or infidel, it has a sacred sanction and controlling force that raises him above all passion, prejudice, or personal bias, lifting him up, so far as nature will allow, into the region of absolute duty and absolute truth— justifying, awing, and ennobling him, binding his conscience and his hopes and fears to the Eternal Conscience and Eternal Power. In the spirit of this majestic oath resting upon your conscience, you are to deliver a *true verdict*, and no other, and therefore do we ask so much attention to the circumstances about to be presented in your hearing."

CONVINCING A JURY

To gain a jury's confidence one need not coax and
flatter them, or beg a verdict, or try to gain favour
by boasting that he knows them by name, or that
they are great business men or plain farmers, and
the like. A better way is to *earn* their confidence
by a full clear statement, and adhering to the merits
unobscured by rubbish and little trifles that clog and
hinder and never produce any real result in arriving
at a verdict.

Men are convinced by fairness, repelled by under-
hand tricks, and led with the sense of justice that
they will expect for themselves To illustrate: A
carpenter sued for extra work and made out his bill
in items. Defendant pleaded payment, but showed
some uncertainty in dates and accounts. The builder
brought his dusty old memorandum-book in pencil,
with day and date of every item. He was very confident it could not deceive him. "Figures don't lie,"
he said to the jury. Counsel followed with his
references to the entry: "If two men weigh grain
and one of the two tallies each hopper full as they
fill it, while the other trusts to his memory, no one
would doubt but the man who kept tally would be
the more reliable. If two men travelled to Europe
and one kept a mile-book, in which he marked each
day's miles made on the journey, eleven days out,
no one would question but he was safer authority
than the one who attempted to remember eleven days
with eleven odd numbers If I have a diary of the
weather for six years every day in every year, I am
safer to speak of the fine days and rainy days of each

season than one who guesses at it. So, in honesty
and justice, tally-sheets tell the whole story better
than many witnesses. Men forget; *books remember*
all that is committed to their keeping. Memory is
uneven, treacherous, uncertain, marks remain change-
less. They are made without motive to falsify; *they
must be truthful.*" This is simple; yet to laymen
is clear common-sense, and they act upon it. The
jury feel a sympathy with the right side. They prefer
to end a controversy according to duty and equity.
They often do better than the Court's instructions.
They strain a point to help out a feeble case for a
deserving client.

What would you have done? is one of the
grandest of reasons in civil and criminal cases. In
Tom Marshall's defence of Matt Ward for shooting
Professor Butler in Louisville before the war, in one
brilliant passage he said: "What would you have
done? What would you have him do under the
circumstances? Stand like a coward, or defend himself?" And Governor Crittenden, following in the
same strain, added (for Ward was not defending
himself, but his brother) · "The law of self-defence
is not so narrow   I am not to defend myself and be
forced to stand by and see my wife, my child, my
helpless ones destroyed. No, gentlemen, if I had no
greater liberty than that, I would *raise my own wild
hand and take this life and hurl it back in the face
of my Maker as a thankless gift.*"

Here was the touch of nature that made all
Kentuckians kin, and won a verdict of acquittal. The
jury *will do right* if they can. So that in criminal
cases, hotly contested, where, for example, the defence
is a home destroyed, all that counsel has to do is

to produce that innate sense of justice, rouse the manhood, and say, *What would you do under the circumstances?* to produce the result and secure acquittal I remember two more instances, one small, one large, in importance. The first was the shooting of a Newfoundland dog in his master's doorway by an excited father who had just rescued his son's bleeding arm from the monster's jaws, and in the heat of passion shot the animal dead, without reflection of when or where In his evidence, on the trial, he said · " I could not help it. I would do it a thousand times, gentlemen. You could not help it. The cry of my boy was like a dagger in my heart. *I had to do it!* "

The other instance was of a newly married man who returned home partly intoxicated and saw through the window a young man act very familiarly with his wife. He hurried in, and was met with a laugh that he did not relish. He ordered the intruder out, and both he and the wife laughed all the louder. He seized the strange man by the arm, but he was much too strong to be handled. This was all done quickly. Turning, he took a piece of stove-wood and felled the man dead at one blow. It was his wife's own brother! But he said "I could not help it, gentlemen. It was a dreadful trial. I was goaded to the heart. It was my impulse. I *was defending my home!* Nothing gets nearer to a jury than such reasoning.

THE "WHITE PAPER RULE."

THREE years ago, having occasion to go from New
York to New Mexico, stopping three days in each
leading city, and making such observations as a
hungry student of human nature will gather of various
men in jury trial practice, I found the following
white paper rule " It easily became apparent that
trial lawyers were not reluctant to relate their rarest
experiences, which, to me, were dense with valuable
information.

It has been a standard rule with many, and should
be written on every lawyer's heart, that the "*good
anywhere should be copied* EVERY*where.*" Acting on
this rule, I often invited strong advocates to name
their best rule of winning cases. The following
came from a Chicago lawyer of national reputation.
"Would you be willing to name your best rule of
practice?" I inquired. "Yes," said the veteran,
"most cheerfully." Taking up two blotters, one full
as it would hold of black ink, and the other clear
white, he commenced ·

"You see that blotter is about as full as it will
hold, don't you?" I nodded assent, and he went on:

"Now, this one (the new one) is free to take ink
readily, and I compare them to every jury. The
average juryman is over forty, and often a super-
visor, always likely to be a man of strong will, whose
mind, once fixed on a subject, is not so easily changed
as before he forms a settled opinion.

"Then the first consideration is, who will get the
most ink on the blotter? When it is once full very
little will stay on. Therefore, when the jury is sworn,

the very first thing for the defence is not to allow all of the surface of the blotter to be saturated with the plaintiff's side without something from the other side I attach great importance to an early and impressive opening and a clear manner of presenting all facts from end to end, the secret of all being—*men will believe what they want to believe and forget what they had rather not remember.*"

To me this was a complete and impressive law lecture, for ink on the blotter is not easily removed

WINNING CASES (No. I.).

THE subject most vital to a trial lawyer's practice is the art of winning cases before juries His record will be early made, and he can govern his fortune for many years by a single victory in a single line of practice With all this responsibility before him, with life and death at his fingers' ends, how few will profit by any other than a series of blunders to attain a reasonable degree of skill in the winning way resorted to by our shrewdest advocates? Some are so selfish that they think they have learned all there is to be known, and need only wait their golden opportunity. As well say one man has seen and owns all the rare paintings in Christendom. The novelty of argument is often the charm that holds a waiting audience. If one expects to win lawsuits before juries —a majority must be won or lost this way—he will early learn the advantage of striking statements and original illustrations.

Mr. Beecher's great popularity grew from his quaint expressions and apt figures of speech, Talmage

came to fame by a similar road; Gough and Collier
each follow the style of speaking that appeals to the
eye and heart and senses, with a unique art that is
captivating.

Lincoln, through his stories, turned many a verdict
that Brady would have won by pathos, Voorhees
by rhetoric, and Webster by a commanding logic.
The history of Corwin's career, with his jokes
excluded, would be mostly unprofitable, Mark Twain,
Bret Harte, and Artemus Ward each establish their
view of the value of *saying something* in speeches.
If we come a little nearer and take a few actual cases,
we will be more firmly grounded in the belief that
saying things with tact, spirit, and energy is the key
to conviction or clearance in very many trials. Here
are three reported instances ·

F. was charged with an assault on E.'s wife with
a stove griddle   He was taken far from his home
and tried by a jury. Deep feeling existed.   Both
families lived in one house, and all knew the unhappy
consequences. For the people, were five witnesses;
for the defence, his own statement. Counsel was
called from a distance, and much expected of his
address to the jury—*simply because he had a name
for making peculiar arguments.* I shall never forget
how serenely he first separated all witnesses, how
clearly he drew the contrast of each story by itself,
how poorly the people's case really matched itself. I
began to think it was time for fine work—when,
without a sign of any notes, counsel began his defence
by the Bible story of " Susanna and the Elders " It
was not over half-told when he was called on to name
the page, and insisted his Bible was not paged, as
every intelligent lawyer should know before his

election as prosecutor! The jury's eyes said, Go on.
They were evidently interested in Susanna's fate, and
we could now see that the spirit of the play was in
the story—when "Daniel come to judgment," and by
his art of separating witnesses released her, counsel
could see that it discharged the defendant, and
abruptly closed his speech with a verdict of acquittal,
and this in the face of *five* witnesses!

The next was an action for trimming shade-trees,
not large in amount, but pointed in practice. M.
owned a house and lot in D., on a corner, near a
planing mill. It was surrounded by tall bushy
shade-trees, forming almost a solid wall of protection
from sparks and fires, quite common at the mill. In
M.'s absence the street shade-trees were closely
trimmed, and a distant relative took the responsibility
of including M.'s corner with the rest, just for the
looks of the street.

The bill was rather unexpected, and accordingly
resisted. A young lawyer defended in this singular
argument, making a full and excellent picture of the
trees and beautiful dwelling, as they originally looked
with limbs and leaves in full size and completeness;
he then sketched the premises, in all their barrenness,
after trimming, and actually made the trees look so
like telegraph-poles, and the house seem so liable to
take fire from exposure to the mill-sparks, that the
point was convincing and complete in the boyish
picture, which he would point to with great confidence, as showing not only *no benefit* (the only
ground, if recovery was had), but a *positive damage
to his client's property*. He wound up a terse and
taking speech by citing the statute on disfiguring
streets by destroying live trees, and won a signal

victory. I have always thought there was more argument in that picture than a two hours' speech would have been to the jury, one of whom remarked: "I have served fifteen years on juries, and never saw a case before so clearly put and illustrated."

The last instance of novelty in argument was in a replevin case to recover to the owner a large black stallion, known as "Black Jack." Simons, the owner, imported him from England. He was very strong, and few could manage him. Being short of money, he was mortgaged for two hundred and fifty dollars, which, when due, was unpaid, but to save suit one hundred dollars more was advanced by the mortgagee for a bill of sale of the animal, granting the vendor possession, use, and income during the current season; it being also agreed that sale should be made at eight hundred dollars, in case of an offer. A lawyer, having a claim in judgment against original owner, levied on the horse, after first securing a written statement as follows:

"I hereby warrant *my horse,* 'Black Jack,' to be seventeen hands high; sound, English blood, seven years old, and that there is no claim against him, *except a mortgage* to *one* Wright, for three hundred and fifty dollars

"Witness, J. WRIGHT   Signed, J SIMONS."

Seeing his horse taken from him, as it were, Wright brought replevin—showed chattel mortgage, bill of sale, identified horse, and rested. The above warranty was then read in evidence, and something proved as to the value of the horse and its inadequate price in the three hundred and fifty dollars, compared with the real value of the property. Plaintiff's case began to look hopeless, as in that state, if the parties intended what they said in the writing, it was a chattel mortgage and no more, even if called a bill of sale. But Wright was recalled, and said he witnessed the paper in a mere formal manner, that the lawyer who asked him to, pretended to be a granger, and did not give him time enough to comprehend the wording he had signed The trial Judge was inclined to call it a mortgage lien, and instructed the jury to find accordingly, before the closing words were said to the jury The ingenious position of plaintiff's counsel was something like this. We agree that Simons imported, owned, mortgaged, and finally sold a large valuable horse to Wright. Here is the horse (a splendid large show picture was exhibited). It was both mortgaged and sold to Wright. It is folly to deny such a statement. Now, if *Wright never sold it back*, then it is unlawful to take *Wright's horse* to pay *Simons' debt*. The bill of sale and mortgage are honestly made and honestly recorded. Could not Wright go, at any time, sell *his* horse to any man? Certainly! Did he sell him to anyone? Never. (Here counsel read sentence by sentence of the " warranty," and said " *that* is not a bill of sale, but a descriptive lie, and does not pass the title to anyone ") " But," continued counsel, " what of the difference in money advanced and value of the horse —the equity side? Why, *this about it*: replevin suits are not in equity, they are suits of *law* to settle legal titles. Men must *make their own* contracts; Courts and juries simply interpret them by common-sense principles. Here was a powerful horse, a man in debt, cramped by a mortgage, allowed, in addition to three hundred and fifty dollars cash, the value of a year's service worth nine hundred dollars more,

think of the certainty of something down—something
to accrue to original owner, and the great risk to
Wright in advancing large sums on such a 'white
elephant' (or black one), that might cast himself,
and die or be disabled any day! Who of the jury
would advance three hundred and fifty dollars even,
and board the horse a year, to get it back? Then,
the price is fair. The horse belongs to Wright, who
never sold it, and is entitled to its possession,"—
which he obtained.

It is this simple style of stating facts that convinces
laymen. In all his arguments, Abraham Lincoln's
art was in his illustrations I remember speaking
with his old neighbours at Springfield, about the year
1870, while his many virtues were fresh in the minds
of all Americans, and all comments on his legal
success pointed to his happy faculty of *utilising
incidents*. One said: "Mr Lincoln was so quaint
that we always expected something; we went to see
him get the jury; he did it handsomely. He never
made any long, dry arguments. His speeches were
crisp, meaty, and full of something to carry home."
Another said "He had a knack of illustrating
his points by some comparison which was always
effective Everything he said had meaning in it, and
was expressed so that it would bring its full meaning
home to the most ignorant person. He was—if I can
use such an expression—the most illustrative man I
ever met in my life. He could illustrate by a jest
or a little anecdote, which would have a volume of
significance."

Winning Cases (No. II)

" Once well done is twice done," makes a good motto in all legal victories. So many cases are poorly tried in the lower Courts that the work is repeated a great many times before it is completed.

The dread of litigation is due to its endlessness and costliness. Lawyers suffer much censure where Courts are to blame, but very often deserve some rebuke for delay growing out of poorly tried cases The difference in skill is like the finish of a painting —the fine art that is paid for most liberally.

Nothing brings business like success. Wealthy clients are the men most willing and able to promote an attorney in practice, and to these he will always appear in one character—either reliable or unreliable They have no time for needless litigation. What they most want is certainty of results and an end of controversy. This is the merchant's practice in his own business, and he prefers promptness and dispatch with others.

In view of what has already been stated, and with an eye single to securing business, no point in practice can be more important than one which secures the right result the earliest I can better illustrate by an actual case lately tried in a Western city, known as " the Reaper Case."

Lockwood was agent for a reaper company, and called on Griffin to sell a high-priced machine early in the harvesting of 1883 Terms being agreed upon, the machine was delivered and set in motion, but the note which was to be given in payment remained not signed—*to be sent on after Griffin's son should try the reaper.*

On a thorough trial, at the end of harvest, Lockwood called for the note and learned that the machine
failed to satisfy the son, and would not be accepted.
Delay past the selling season, and disappointment
generally, created much feeling between the parties,
and either stood ready to fight the other through
the highest Court to the last ditch, if need be, for
justice. At such a time trial lawyers too often partake
of the spirit and bad blood of the contestants. In
this case great bitterness was shown, up to the
drawing of the jury, when, by adroitness of counsel,
it suddenly changed to a more friendly contest   The
evidence pointed to a sale and delivery with a slight
condition of reserve to suit, or should satisfy the
buyer's son. This condition being made mainly on
defendant's testimony and the sale by plaintiff's agent,
the case turned on a wire, as we say, either way,
plaintiff or defendant. The jury gave defendant the
benefit of the doubt *Whether the minds ever fully
met on one thing at one time and constituted an
absolute contract*

Defendant's counsel confined his evidence and
argument to this simple inquiry, and with the best
of temper praised the truthfulness of all witnesses,
eulogised reapers, extolled their agents, and enlarged
upon the growth of improvements; insisted the reaper
was one of the best, but the sale had a condition,
and the buyer sought to enforce it. The jury,
thinking their turn might come some time, found
for the defendant But the effect of good humour
or the high compliment paid the reaper induced the
agent to take it back, pay the costs, and end all
trouble "That is the kind of litigation," said
a listener, "that would make lawyers more re-

spected." How differently would a little abuse have resulted!

Chauncey Schaffer, now of New York, tells of his early experience when lawyers were paid in boots and shoes, or produce, before large fees were dreamed of. He lived in Western Michigan, and John Van Arman, his senior, practised law at Marshall, in the same county. One day an excited shoemaker retained Schaffer—or agreed to—in an insult case, then adjourned for a week, to come off before a jury. Schaffer was to travel twelve miles and be ready early, and do his best, and not let up on his opponent, but "everlastingly pummel him before the jury" He was to receive two pairs of boots in payment for his services. He had not heard the case nor seen the witnesses, but was to call early enough to learn the circumstances.

On the trial day young Schaffer was early on the ground and ready for action, when to his chagrin the defendant had hired Van Arman, now of Chicago, and decided he needed no more counsel. Schaffer was indignant. It was his first case He had studied a week and dreamed of it nights till it seemed a part of his being. No one appreciates this better than one who has been talked out of a case on the ground of being too young and inexperienced.

He finally asked for one pair of boots, and he would go home. This was refused, and Schaffer said, "You are unreasonable—you deserve to be defeated," and said it with such emphasis that the prosecutor invited him to take a retainer on the other side, and by consent Schaffer remained in case for the people.

The trial came on after dinner. Van Arman opened rather strongly, followed by others, with

5

Schaffer to close   He was large, boyish, and timid, but powerful in his personal convictions.   He eulogised Van Arman's effort, and said only two reasons prevented it from carrying the jury and securing an acquittal: *one was the clear guilt of the defendant, and the other his treatment of his chosen counsel'* (Sensation.) He went on and graphically related the story of the defendant's guilt, and turned to his "secondly" with all the fervour of a Methodist bishop, and with the naturalness of an actor told how he had been retained and "studied the case day and night, and finally was discarded and about to be defrauded of his boots for the winter, and have his maiden effort burn in his brain, unknown and unheard by his schoolmates and neighbours!" The jury were now fairly electrified.   "And such is the character of the man who provoked this quarrel—provoked me—provoked us all—and attempted to swindle this community out of the ablest effort of my life!"

With much more of this line, young Schaffer played upon the minds of his delighted hearers for an hour, amid cheers for his wit and sarcasm, till the whole Court room gave assent to this theory and the jury said "Guilty." The Court fined defendant $100.

Schaffer never won a finer victory. He is now nearly seventy, vigorous and hearty, but this was his start in practice. The suit broke up in a row where some forty quarrelled in the bar-room, and it is said that defendant really got an extra beating in the last scuffle. The lesson is a clear one   Win your cases honourably and treat your opposing counsel fairly. It makes business

Winning Cases (No. III)

When Dr. Agnew made his skilful opening in General Garfield's side, relieved the pain, and let the world breathe freer by a single act, thousands applauded science. That science was experience When Graham cleared McFarland for shooting Richardson in the *Tribune* office in '72, people said "So much for sham insanity." Graham's act was experience. When Ford was acquitted recently in Missouri, men murmured at the ignorance of juries.

Time has demonstrated that General Garfield's doctors were skilful, but science was most decidedly wanting. All of the instruments were deceptive on the location of the bullet, on its direction, and the extent of the injury.

The public were behind the age in the McFarland case, as every important murder trial since has clearly shown. And to-day it is a noted fact that no jury can be found to convict a man or woman well defended, who has taken life in defence of their home and fireside—especially where one has punished the destroyer of his wife's virtue, and the family were shown to live happy before the victim meddled with forbidden fruit. Laws are not strong enougn, statutes not binding enough, to stay a husband's hand in this species of self-defence. Juries know it, and lawyers realise it everywhere.

As to the acquittal of Ford, something of prejudice may have crept into the jury box, but the real cause of the verdict was a *lack of belief in the people's evidence* There was a general over-confidence that is the means of losing many cases.

People were too sanguine of skill in Garfield's case and over-confident in the Ford case.

There is a common disposition to underrate our enemies. Lawyers too often, on the statement of clients, assume that there is no defence, or that there is no *other side* to the question. Defeat lurks along this line always; success lies in a different direction.

It is well to assume that the jury will hear the other side, that they will see any weakness in your witnesses, and balance the evidence. That which is fairest produces most justice, facts given with the most candour, enforced by the clearest circumstances, will capture the common-sense of a jury.

To be convinced of this fact, spend a half-hour with some good juryman fresh from a well-contested suit in which you were defeated. He will teach you more than a law lecture. He will show you that you have much to learn on the subject of clearness, much to prove that you took for granted.

If counsel will note down and preserve for a dozen years the rare points of practice, and the daily little victories in Courts under his immediate notice, he will profit very greatly by the habit. If law journals, like medical monthlies, would tally and preserve for reference the strange incidents, and their application to daily trials in every State, it would form a fund of information invaluable in practice. This must be the end and object of more in the profession before we shall profit by the wisdom of experience. There is no patent on such knowledge. It is no injury to a lawyer in Ohio that one in Kentucky has found his best rule in practice. There is very little danger of rivalry between counsel, and all that is done in an open Court room is public property, for the public benefit.

I have often observed how carefully all special cases in medicine or surgery are kept and reported in the interest of science, and I predict that within a score of years the science of law will copy this valuable practice; and more than this—the power and influence of well-managed evidence in trials of fact before juries will become a branch of study next in importance to elementary principles. . . .

Robert Toombs and Alexander Stephens once contested a suit growing out of a doctor's bill that is very instructive, as well as amusing. After proving the number and value of the visits, Toombs rested, and Stephens told his client the case was clearly made out for plaintiff and left no room for defence.

Defendant was greatly displeased, and followed by saying, " I hired you to speak, and I want you to speak." " But," rejoined Stephens, " there is nothing to be said " " Then," said the stubborn client, " if Bobby Toombs won't be too hard on me, I'll speak " Toombs said he would not, and Peter proceeded (I abbreviate slightly from original report):

" Gentlemen of the jury, you and I is plain farmers, and if we don't stick together these lawyers and doctors will get the advantage of us. I ain't no lawyer or doctor, and I ain't no objection to them in their proper place, but they ain't farmers, gentlemen of the jury. Now, this man Royston was no doctor, and I went for him to doctor my wife's sore leg, and he put some salve on it and some rags, but never done it a bit of good. I don't believe he is a doctor anyway. There are doctors, sure enough, but this man don't earn his money; and if you send for, him, as Mrs. Sarah Atkinson did for a negro boy worth $1,000, he just kills him and wants you to pay it."

"I don't," thundered the doctor.

"Did you cure him?" asked Peter, with the slow accents of a Judge with a black cap on. The doctor was silent, and Peter proceeded: "As I was saying, gentlemen of the jury, we farmers, when we sell our cotton, go to give value for the money we ask, and doctors ain't none too good to be put to the same rule. And I don't believe this Sam Royston is a doctor nohow."

"Look at my diploma, if you think I am no doctor."

"His diploma!" exclaimed the orator, with great contempt. "His diploma! Gentlemen, that is a big word for printed sheepskin, and it don't make no doctor of the sheep as first wore it, nor does it of the man as now carries it, a good newspaper has more in it, and I show you that he ain't no doctor at all."

The doctor was now in a fury, and screamed out: "Ask my patients if I am not a doctor"

"I asked my wife," retorted Peter. "She said she thought he was not."

"Ask my other patients," said the doctor.

This seemed to be the straw that broke the camel's back, for Peter replied with a look and tone of unutterable sadness "That is a hard saying, gentlemen of the jury, and one that requires me to die, or to have powers ceased to be exercised since the Apostles. Does he expect me to bring the Angel Gabriel down before his time and cry aloud, 'Awake, ye dead, and tell this Court and jury your opinion of Sam Royston's practice?' Am I to go to the lonely

churchyard and rap on the silent tomb and say to
them at rest from physic and doctors' bills, ' Rise up
here, you, and state if you died a natural death, or
was hurried on by the doctors?' He says, Ask his
patients; and, gentlemen of the jury, *they are all
dead!* Where is Mrs. Beasley's man, Sam? Go ask
the worms in the graveyard, where he lies Mr. Peak's
woman, Sarah, was attended by him, and her funeral
was appointed, and he, the doctor, had the corpse
ready. Where is the likely Bill that belonged to
Mr. Mitchell? Gone in glory expressing his opinion
of Royston's doctoring. Where is that baby of
Harry Stevens'? She is where doctors cease to
trouble and the infants are at rest. Gentlemen, he
has eaten chickens enough at my house to pay for
this salve. I found the rags, and I don't suppose he
charges for making her worse; and even he don't
pretend to charge for curing her, and I am humbly
thankful that he never gave her nothing, as he did
his other patients, for something made 'um all die
mighty sudden "

The applause was great. The doctor lost, and
Peter won.

Winning Cases (No. IV.).

Courage in Court —A very brilliant defence was
made by General Rousseau, in Louisville, in 1857,
where a remarkable trial was conducted with a spirit
and energy seldom witnessed It appears, as reported
by Harper Brothers, that a family of six persons
named Joyce were murdered, and their bodies burned
near the city.

Suspicion fell on some negroes of an adjoining

plantation, who were seized, threatened, and hung up until half dead and a confession sought to be gained, but was refused One was tied to a stake and a fire kindled near him, when he, to avoid burning, confessed that himself and the others committed the murder. They were arrested and placed in gaol to await their trial. The master believed them innocent, and retained Rousseau; no other counsel could be retained

The excitement was tremendous. The undertaking of such a defence single-handed was brave and courageous. Many of the general's friends urged him not to sacrifice his popularity by siding with such debased criminals. Rousseau replied, "The greater the guilt the greater the need of a good lawyer to defend them," and said· he did not believe in confessions extorted in that manner Then many cursed him openly as an "Abolitionist." The trial brought a crowded Court room. The sole survivor of the Joyce family sat inside the railing, with a crowd of his friends just outside the bar. The feeling of an outbreak was only restrained by a certainty of conviction. But the excitement was painful, and fears of a momentary outbreak prevailed.

Rousseau's conduct was prompt and daring. The confession of the tortured negro was the people's sole evidence. He told in a hesitating way how the murder had been committed and the house fired in several places. That after it was encircled in flames, the youngest child, a girl of two years, had been overlooked: now aroused by the light, called to her mother to know if she was cooking breakfast. A death-like stillness followed, when one of the jurymen, shading his face with his hands, muttered "Tut,

tut, tut!" in a half-hissing sound heard over the
Court room A cold shudder ran through the
crowd, and in the excitement young Joyce sprang
to his feet and said excitedly, "*I want my friends
who think these negroes guilty to help me to hang
them.*" A wild shout and clear clicking of pistols
was his answer. Joyce drew his knife from a sheath
and sprang towards the prisoners. Rousseau caught
him by the throat with one hand and clasped the
wrist with the other, thrust him back to his seat, and
confronted the crowd with the aid of two policemen. The crowd made a rush in the direction, and
Rousseau said, "Tell your friends, Mr. Joyce, while
they attend to the negroes I'll attend to you" Joyce
waved his friends back, and the Judge ordered
policemen to aid the sheriff to protect the Court and
keep order. "Don't do that, your Honour," said
counsel, "we can protect the law and its officers.
There are enough true men to protect the prisoners
from mob violence." "Who are your friends?"
cried the furious crowd. "You are," said Rousseau.
Then he turned, and in burning words told them to
protect the young man from committing a crime
which would forever disgrace them as a law-abiding
community The crowd calmed down and said,
"He's right! He's right!"

The trial proceeded quietly to the close, when the
verdict of "Not guilty" was given amidst terrible
excitement. The prisoners had been removed in
time to secure protection. But the people would
have blood, and the same night a mass of men surrounded the gaol, removed the prisoners, and hung
them to trees in the grounds of the city hall. Mayor
Pelcher was hit by a missile and died from the injury.

In several trials Rousseau defended negroes from aiding guilty parties in escaping from slavery—then a high crime in Kentucky. But few men could bear such a character. He later became a senator, and famous as a general, and later was employed to assist in a famous case—the trial of Jeff Davis for treason.

This is the same kind of bravery that Seward showed in the Freeman case. Denounced as he was for defending a negro who had killed the Van Ness family, he believed in the prisoner's innocence, or insanity, and followed his case, after defeat, to the Court of Appeals, where a reversal was secured, and pending a new trial Freeman died in gaol. His brain was examined and found to be actually rotten.

Cases of courage in the Court room would fill a volume of rare reading. They are known in almost every State. But I have seldom known of greater courage than that shown by the late Senator Jacob M. Howard, who, while prosecuting in the great conspiracy case, became convinced of the innocence of the accused (forty men for attempting to burn the Michigan Central Railroad bridge at Niles), said, "It is enough for counsel to deprive one of his property or rob him of character in a contest for his client, but when it comes to taking away his liberty for years (which is in effect his life) and depriving his kindred of his protection, while his memory is branded with the stigma of a felon's name, it is far more creditable and honourable to lose a case, and go to one's judgment hereafter without the tarnish of human blood on his garments for committing a higher crime than the accused was charged with."

TEN TRIAL RULES.

THE selection and proper treatment of a jury should be classed as one of the fine arts. It is a thing very difficult to do properly: a life of close observation and active practice, with a natural adaptability, are required for its mastery. The writer, in his recent work on "Trial Practice," gives "Ten Trial Rules" which are here quoted:

1. Select young jurymen, with warm intelligent faces; exclude officers of every kind. Become early familiar with the winning facts of both sides. Conceal them, and instruct parties and witnesses to keep silent and let the counsel do the planning of theories.

2 Find what opponents are likely to prove and how probable will be the showing, and. if false, how it can be denied or met by fair explanation.

3. Nothing takes so well as common-sense. Be reasonable. Never weary a Court with technicalities, nor a jury with quibbles, nor offend a witness by browbeating, but know what you need to make a case and stop when it is established, so that the jury may see the sharp end of your evidence.

4. Cross-examine only with an object—bring out the point and don't cover it. Avoid all abuse of counsel or parties; such quarrels draw attention from the issue and cause disagreements, while kindness and fair play win a lasting victory.

5. Explain the reason of the law to the jury, or in their hearing. The average mind is wiser than many suppose. But be sure the jury know the consequences of the verdict.

6. Counsel, and not clients, should control cases and trials.

7. In opening an argument, select first the points on which there is least dispute, and, if possible, those nearest with your position. Pass to the others with confidence, and carry the jury with you by reason, not by threats, not by bombast. Leave appeals until after the convincing is accomplished But feel what you say, and believe what you say, always.

8. Treat a jury with unbounded confidence, like begets like, under all circumstances. Men are not driven by threats, but persuaded and convinced by reason and common-sense when it is clearly illustrated. Jurymen prefer to do right. Shew them the right road in a plain and clear manner.

9. The strongest reason is: What would you have done under like circumstances? Human nature finds excuses for wrongs that lead to good results and are justifiable. Men generally do on a jury what seems most reasonable, if it is shewn to them in a sensible and convincing manner

10. There is no opportunity better than the earliest. Let the jury know from the beginning that you believe in your rights and will fairly enforce them, while their minds are as clear as *white* paper. "Write it on their hearts and engrave it on their bones" that your client has the rights you contend for and will ask for none other. But insist upon justice On this be so full, so determined, so fortified with law and reasonable evidence, that it will stand like a mountain, unshaken either by quibbles or appeals.

SELECTING COUNSEL.

The wisdom of a Chancery lawyer may be lost
with a jury. It is a very common fault with speakers
to reason over the heads of their hearers. For this
reason the country pettifogger outwits the wiser
counsel from a large city. This is mainly done by
ridicule Very few juries have the stamina to with-
stand ridicule when woven into a closing argument,
and the only way to meet it is by an open analysis
in advance of the final speaker. If adroitly done,
this method is effective.

In a case of a couple of orphans against an
insurance company the selection of counsel was left
to the executor, who did it with rare discretion. The
closing of the trial seemed to indicate a decided
defeat of the claim, which was one of a series,
amounting to $20,000, and counsel's services in such
cases are not easily over-estimated.

The case lawyer was extremely rasping and
unpleasant in opening, and dwelt upon the technical
grounds almost tediously. He was followed by two
pleasing speakers on plausible theories, and the
homely speaker permitted to sum up the plaintiff's
case in two hours after dinner. Nothing in his
appearance spoke for him. Nothing of his voice had
been heard in side-discussions. He was reserved,
like the racehorse at the county fair, to make a
superior heat to the spectators.

I can see him as he stood up timidly, age over
seventy, tall, uncouth, awkward, clear Scotch accent,
with a ring to it like a triangle in a band He began
low and full, and grew deeper. Men that had

turned down the stairway as they saw him rise to speak, turned back to catch the soft rhythmical sentences, measured and low and charged with meaning, and one by one crept back on the benches and listened The room was hushed as at a funeral. I had decided to go with the rest, but was spellbound at the opening sentence that soon followed, which was pronounced by the late William A. Beach to be the most touching period he ever read of any American argument. I let the words tell their own story Raising his eyes to the ceiling, he stood like one transfixed in awe and majesty, and said · "Oh! I can see her now, it is early twilight, it is winter, the snow is falling fast and slippery, whitening the little plank-walk to the cistern. She has company; she hurries down the walk, catching up a pail, leaving the hook hanging over the curbing, bending low, she slips, she falls, the water covers her, no one hears, she is drowned! It is an accident, and I almost hear her say, as she looks down to you, to this upright Judge, this honest jury · 'Gentlemen, you may cheat my children, if you will, but spare them the burden of dishonour · the money will be a poor pittance at the most to that priceless character that my innocent children should inherit ' We plead for the money that they deserve, we plead for the character that they own, we plead for the justice that their evidence demands; make their lives happy and their mother's memory sweet—sweet as the day she bade them good-night—the night before the night of death—little dreaming of the sudden end, little dreaming of the scandal they should meet, little dreaming she should be held up in horror to frighten a jury from duty—held up in shame, and

deceased to blot out the fair name she had earned
for her children! You will not stain these little ones,
gentlemen—you will not pay a claim that way, you
will not cancel a just debt by a mean insinuation
of wrong? Why, gentlemen, they would have you
think that this woman loved her little ones so much
that she dared the pains of hell and drowned herself
that they might be made rich, though orphaned!
No crown of glory she held in prospect, no garland
of the blessed to be wreathed upon her brow!—only
a sordid fraud, a leap in the dark oblivion of the
great hereafter, to get gain!

*   *   *   *   *

"Gentlemen, my work is almost done, poor as it
is. I must trust to you to do a better work. And
my little clients" (here the speaker laid one hand on
each client's shoulder, and amid the hushed silence
of rapt attention, said)—"my little clients, may God
bless you! I have done my best to make your
name an honour to our State. But oh, how poor and
weak my words have been! And you, gentlemen,
even now, by your silence and interest in this case,
methinks I hear you say. Stop! Delay no longer!
Let us begin this work of justice! Stop! that we
may restore these orphans to their own—to that
pure character that they will love to honour—a
character as pure as they knew her on that last and
long good-night. Stop! that you may wipe away
all tears from these orphan eyes and plant the sweet
rose of a mother's love in their bright young lives,
to grow, bloom, and bless the world for their living
in it. Stop! that we may right this wrong at once.
O God! put it into the hearts of this jury to see

the truth—to vindicate a mother's name and a mother's love to her helpless children.

" O God ! remove the mist of this case, reveal the truth to these jurors, let them see their duty and give them strength to do right, and do it, remembering that some day—yes, an early day to most of them— when they shall be called home to leave, it may be, dependent children and a sacred memory of a good name, that of future juries they may expect the same just finding that they have found for us—a verdict and a vindication."

Jury found $5,300, and the other three cases were duly paid. The case was an ideal jury trial. I have reported it from memory.

.

THE LUCK OF LAWYERS.

Confucius says, " The archer who misses the centre of the target turns to himself to find the cause of his failure " He was a wise teacher.

A lawsuit is such a costly luxury to either party that failure becomes an important matter. One would often pay the expenses of both sides to be sure of being a winner in the contest.

It is so humiliating to be defeated that great anxiety follows a litigation from beginning to end. But to fail on a trifling lack of evidence—a thing that can seldom ever be supplied after the failure— is a bitter disappointment, and must lead one to *look to himself !*

It is not possible to win all cases, and hardly probable that over half, taken as they come, will stand the test of a higher Court's review. But of the sorted cases a large majority should be reasonably certain in results. For this reason, wise and expensive counsel are engaged to watch every turn and insure a victory. These are often no more certain than alert and artful young lawyers.

As Court victories generally lead to an increase of business and wider reputation, while losing cases will often ruin a good law practice, to win is highly essential to success.

Reputation for tact or eloquence usually begins in the Bar and extends throughout the county, then the State, and possibly the nation, or even becomes worldwide by the importance of the controversy.

But no matter what one's talents are or what his ability to try cases may be, if he has an inland city practice and no cases of public interest he may remain for a lifetime in a narrow range of practice. So the luck of a lawyer is his class of cases, success in Court, and location of business A New Yorker has twenty to one chances over a man in a Kansas Court room to be known as successful. This is a large element of greatness—the notice that is taken of his trials and triumphs, and the attention that such victories deserve.

This is not intended to make everyone start on the keen run for New York to begin practice—not by any means. You may be a thousand times better off where you are The metropolis is already overcrowded with advocates. Governors of States, generals of armies, senators, and wealthy men of national renown and brilliant talents are there before you. They are established and, like the great daily papers, have their patronage that newly made ventures will hardly disturb. As well might all editors start for a large city who now enjoy a fine income at home, and there would be likely to starve.

But it may be noted that lawyers and newspapers of real merit and originality will command attention wherever located, and in like proportion to their tact, skill, and eloquence will attain to eminence. All things come to those who work and wait.

STARTING IN LAW.

THE study of law to a beginner is like entering a dark tunnel—the start is always the darkest. Gradually light breaks in, and soon it seems like daylight. This is due to the fact that it seems a large undertaking. It is large   It *is* dark.

To one who has been across the continent several times the journey appears much shorter, and to one who sees far enough to know the reason of rules, maxims, and definitions, and the object of knowing them, and their use and application to principles involved in trials, and how verdicts are controlled, a greater relish is given to the different branches of study used in explaining these principles

It is not right to try a short cut through law studies, for there is none   But sometimes, like a surveyor's measure of a lake, we may be guided by two angles to find the other, and tell much that is essential and useful from one outside point to another.

All mystery should be omitted at the beginning. The plainest facts should be stated with their illustrations, and simple principles gathered in little groups like familiar stories should be dwelt upon to

feed the mind, interest the reader, and open little
doors first to that part of the law which leads directly
into the office and Court room. This should be done
to incite a lively interest in the theme and its
requirements.

Instead of this method, we find nearly every
student first put at copying, or reading Blackstone—
one of the heaviest law works of all history, and
especially so to a very young student All admit
that Blackstone is the basement-storey of law practice.
But all are not sure that one in beginning will find
interest in Blackstone. As well place a student of ten
years to the study of Shakespeare.

The start in law is always an experiment Early
enough, if interested and gifted, will the young man
be led to know that he must build on such authors,
but the *start* in law should be made more gradual
by becoming familiar with the range of study, and
to this end some clever counsel should talk over the
books in half-day lectures, and thoroughly and early
impress the beginner with their use and reason, as
the object of his undertaking. It will be well to say
something encouraging of the wide fields surrounding
so dense and dismal a forest through which one
must go long and fatiguingly to find the high prizes
of promotion.

INCIDENTS IN ARGUMENT.

It is said of Chief Justice Coleridge, of England, that he was first heard of through a famous murder trial, in which, while he was closing to the jury, the lights went out, and when re-lighted he added the forcible words. "The life of the prisoner is in your hands, gentlemen. You can extinguish it as easily as that candle was extinguished but a moment since, but it is not in your power to restore that life once taken as that light has been restored " The argument won.

So an obscure writer first attracted the attention of a London editor by the graphic description of "A Night in the Thames Tunnel," and, being sent for, admitted that, lacking lodging money, he paid his penny fare and stayed out the long hours with other like destitutes. He was placed in an Edinburgh printing-place—£200 a year—and a few years later created a sensation by his "Life in London," that had a marvellous sale. The incidents in these arguments called attention to their brilliancy, his genius and capacity.

Mr. Moody's description of the millionaire prisoner in Ohio penitentiary, after thirty-three years of confinement, of his long persistent quarrel with a railroad company in the Courts (for crossing his farm) and anger at defeat, and his placing an obstruction on the track one dark night that threw off the train and killed several persons, and his final conviction and life sentence; and a few years later of his finding a thriving city grown up on his farm, divided by his supposed enemy, the railway track; of his being made a very wealthy man by it, yet left a miserable captive within prison walls,—was intensified by the fact that Moody had personally known the prisoner and learned the story from his heartbroken language.

The same speaker, who is a model in making arguments of incidents, tells of a Chicago defaulter in a county office, who a few years ago concealed himself from the law officers and remained day after day secreted in his own city. Night after night he would steal into his family room, walk silently past the sleeping children, fearing to wake them lest they should tell their schoolmates and reveal his hiding-place; and at last he woke them with his farewell kisses, surrendered, pleaded guilty, and was sentenced to nineteen years' imprisonment. Moody tells it, directly from the prisoner, with graphic power and marvellous effectiveness.

It is not so much the story told, as the fitness and timely application, that convinces. The little touching references to the surroundings of a story, like the kissing of his children in the dark and his creeping as by stealth to take a last look, are touches of nature to awaken emotions in all hearers.

I remember talking to a Texas lawyer who enforced this lesson most keenly by a point in his personal experience, which I once related with effect in a different kind of case, and this is the pith of it (for in all articles I write with a narrow column and limited space ever before me) "I was thinking," he said, "how I could bring home to the jury the fact that long imprisonment means death, when I thought of the long trial we were engaged in and their own anxiety for release, and I said, 'You that have been

from home but a month on this jury, how the days
have dragged on, how the nights have seemed long
and weary, how you have longed for a sight of the
old farmhouse. of your cattle, of your wife, of your
little girls and boys, who are even now wondering
what keeps father so long away on the jury! But
how short it is compared to fourteen years of twelve
long months each—five thousand days and five
thousand nights   alone in prison, without hope,
without comfort, without pure air, without family,
without freedom! Such endurance is worse than
death. It is a million deaths! "

He won by it.

FRIENDS AND MONEY.

A GOOD bank account is a means of creating
courage, confidence, and business. It is kept good
by careful investments and not drawing out quite
all that is deposited. One had better charge less and
collect cash and bank it than keep open client
accounts—they go elsewhere while in your debt and
care very little about past services.

It is a great loss to lawyers if suits are brought
without foundation. Far more cases come to office
than deserve to be placed in Court, and a very sure
test in sorting out the good from bad ones is by
asking a large retainer on doubtful cases, stating it is
for the very reason that they are doubtful, and require
more attention.

The client who says he has a good case is too
much interested to decide on a matter of that nature.
About half that he says is not capable of proof under

the strict rules of evidence, and one-quarter of that may be denied by the other side, and leave the case rather slender. He will weaken if the advance cash is considerable.

To avoid offending the other side uselessly will double one's business in the long run, while offence given to please one client will react in many instances. The client you appear for may not always be such, and the adversary may be in position to judge of your unfairness if attempted. But never try to please both sides except by doing right.

Claim about as much for your side as can be shown by circumstances—neither too little nor too much. Else by overreaching you create distrust, and by under-estimate you weaken confidence. Men are so human that they will not over-credit poor humanity. Still you must win. Your fees depend on victory well earned and fairly won.

Fairness is such a jewel in practice that every trial increases its brightness. The man that juries take to is one who soon makes business through popularity. If a hundred men all say something good of a lawyer—and one new one each week—he will not long remain poor or lacking in cases.

The man that *carries his heart into cases* is the one who convinces others by sincerity, and once in the possession of public confidence he may look for his share of its patronage. Estates and financial interests fall to the lot of the worthy, and affections cling to the successful and diligent.

To use others as we would be used by them may sound odd and simple, but no better motto has ever been invented on earth or from heaven. It is a rule of business that makes character; and what is great riches with a soiled reputation?

The boys that grow up around us are the men of the future. They start from college with a longing to be either wealthy like Bliss, eloquent like Beach, or great like Webster A passing word will help them. They will return it many times in giving you a good name and deserved honour.

In the long run of trade, business, and professional life, the one great rule will govern most people, and that is seldom ever considered; it is this. "*Success in life, in anything, depends upon the number to whom one can make oneself agreeable.*"

TO CROSS-EXAMINE WELL.

THINK first what an icy pavement you tread upon, think how a willing witness may say too much that had been unproved without him; think how the rivet may be clinched and the strength redoubled by facts too often repeated and committed to memory; think how you may develop new theories for your adversary, and act with quiet discretion.

The art of cross-examination is to shew a conflict of testimony. It may not be successful, yet, if skilfully worded, it will convince some on the panel that you have at least moral evidence of the facts aimed to be established. It is not the place to exhibit smartness, that will be better if concealed. To entrap a false witness, to confuse a timid one, to encourage one who will aid your theory, are good uses of this high art.

Most young lawyers think they appear dull if they pass a witness without " tearing him to pieces " under rigid questioning, and find that they have fed their enemy at every question. Older advocates use this weapon with tact and caution. They have tried the sabre exercise too often, and remember the deep scars it produced on their clients.

Three kinds of witnesses may be shaken by cross-questions · (1) Those who swear recklessly; (2) those who swear defiantly; and (3) those who swear falsely. The last named may be impeached, if he fails to impeach himself, by his own story. Only a few persons can continue long in telling falsehoods without detection.

The fine art of cross-examining is in making your case out of an opponent's witness This is almost always done by a gentle and delicate leading process, coupled with a concealed kindness that fascinates and encourages, while it creates the reasonable doubt or supplies the broken thread of a story that you are seeking to establish.

Of all men puzzled by cross-questions doctors are the most pliable. They deal in strange phrases and queer theories, and out of twenty or thirty ten will admit that all men are at times a little unanchored in intellect. They will swear through a series of vivid dreams, temporary insanity caused by jealousy, or prolonged litigation, by a quiet and well-followed invitation.

There are no better rules of cross-examination than five: (1) Know what you need, and stop when you get it (2) Risk no case on the hazard of an answer that may destroy it (3) Hold your temper while you lead the witness, if convenient, to lose his. (4) Ask as if wanting one answer when you desire the opposite, if the witness is against you; and reverse the tactics if he is more tractable. (5) Treat a witness like a runaway colt; and see that he does not get too much the start of his master; and if he does, let go of the reins at the first safe turn in the testimony; but if you see any object to break his running, call the turn quickly.

THE GET-READY RULE.

THE late Judge Curtis, of Boston, gave hints as a basis for the following trial rules that are not so generally known as they should be, and yet they very forcibly apply to criminal defences:

1. Pay little attention to the good side of the case at first—that side will take care of itself; but be sure you look well to the bad side, not forgetting to explore the strongest form of the proof, and knowing that an opportunity to prove even what is false may be used by your adversary unless you have certain means to refute it.

2 Never try to disprove what has not been proven, and supply thereby the missing link in the enemies' chain of evidence.

3 Never forget that an innocent person with enemies may be in a more dangerous condition than a guilty one with friends and influence.

4. The pulse of the people beat nearest together through the columns of the Press, and a few wicked papers may tell a jury much in half-hour accounts of an occurrence that will shade the whole story by it unawares.

5 Persistent energy in the face of genius and eloquence will bear its fruit in due season if properly

directed, but endless travel in the wrong direction will never reach the place of destination; therefore, of all things, be safe in your theory and start out equipped for a trial of hardship.

Chas. S. May, of Kalamazoo, Mich., says: " The best trial rule I can think of is for the advocate first to possess himself thoroughly of the facts of his case, and to believe in its justice, and then to keep in mind in every step of its progress that the jury is composed of men representing the average common-sense and moral sense of the people, actuated by an honest desire to do impartial justice between the parties, and so, in the light of this fact, to be able to see how every proposition or objection, piece of testimony, remark at the Bar or observation from the Bench, would be likely to affect such a body, in other words, for the trial lawyer to imagine himself in the jury-box, with their purposes and intelligence, and think how these things would be apt to influence him "

OUTSIDE PRESSURE.

WHILE the earliest reasoners used fables and allegories, the latest employ all the arts of argument in the one method of claiming to be in the majority. Public popularity is invoked to win with.

That the greatest body of men ever called to decide a given question should be governed by this reason is shown in the verdict of the famous electoral commission, and the recent Ohio Scott liquor-law discussion, for what other reason could govern such eminent and learned tribunals than a desire to be with their party and sustain its arguments?

It is not so certain to-day that important questions are even so elaborately argued as they were in the primitive stages of our country's history; but it is a solemn fact that, with a community set for or against a case, the result will either be like the verdict of that community or a spiteful disagreement.

It is not a time when men are aroused like the listeners to Mark Antony's funeral oration, or Cicero's appeal for Gavius, where a few well-chosen words created a radical change of sentiment. Men were then moved by simple reasons, now they are their own judges of the results of verdicts.

Following in this modern line of argument were the great trials of McFarland-Richardson, the Sickles-Key, Newland-Evans, and the Buford-Elliot cases, that were all decided in accord with public opinion and outside pressure.

But a few exceptions, like the Webster-Parkman and Beecher-Tilton trials, varied a little from this general rule, with the ablest efforts the great advocate, Wm H Seward, failed to bend the custom in the case of the demented negro whom he defended. Public opinion insisted upon his conviction, and the opinion was enforced—even with a brain so diseased that it parted like earth at the touch of the post-mortem examiner's knife.

That public opinion will yield to persistent argument was shown in the Buford case named, where the feeling that would once have lynched him became a sentiment of sympathy and compassion later on in the contest A more radical change of feeling has seldom been recorded than the release of this slayer of "the Mountain King."

From these brief references it will appear quite
vital to success in argument that every person charged
with an offence at law should be tried by an impartial
jury, in an unbiased community, and by counsel who
can comprehend the use of weapons that secure fair
play and even-handed justice; for without these
advantages no honest victory is probable   It is not on
the rumour of the populace, nor on the evidence of
enemies, nor where truth is perverted, that a jury
should weigh testimony and arrive at a just verdict.
but by an unbiased and independent judgment

CONDUCT IN COURT.

I NEVER knew but one man in Court who quite
filled all expectations as to what a lawyer should do
before a jury, and that man is no longer with the
minority   full of honour, and the idol of many
admirers, he has passed to his reward, which I hope
is as beautiful as his career was brilliant.

It was in June, 1873, that I chanced to hear and
see him, and I shall not soon forget the lasting
impression.   He was of medium size—five feet nine in
height, weighing, say, one hundred and sixty-five
pounds; very erect, warm face smoothly shaven, a
small beard on the chin, large head nearly bald, with
long, thin, silver-grey hair worn much like an
Englishman.   His tone was deep and thrilling.   His
arms and hands moved gracefully, yet with an earnest
rugged grace all unstudied   His whole manner was
respectful, eloquent, sublime.

He was an ideal advocate.   Voice better than
Carpenter's, sentences more thrilling, bearing more

dignified. Not so learned as Evarts, not so strong
as Webster, not so brilliant as Brady, but a strong
combination of all their general qualities woven into
one great lawyer.

I see him now as he sat near a young beardless
junior, taking notes rapidly, when an opposing
counsel objected too often, and the Court rebuked it
Rising in a respectful way, he said, "I *thank* your
Honour." The melody of his voice was beautiful.
Once more I hear a point made by counsel: "What
we insist is, that there is no evidence of marriage."
Instantly he is alert! Commencing slowly, while
rising to his feet, he said: "Evidence of marriage!
What is evidence of marriage? Why, living together.
may it please your Honour! Cohabiting together,
may it please your Honour! Introducing each other
as husband and wife, raising up children together,
may it please your Honour! For all these relations
they were married! Ay, that going down into the very
valley and shadow of death that a woman assumes in
such relations—they were married! They were married when he enjoyed the bloom of her youth and
her heart's loving tenderness—married when it flattered his vanity to enjoy her beauty, but when we
come to that other time, when of all times marriage
is most sacred, when they should be leading each
other down the western slope of life's steep hillside,
to rest together at the foot, *in long repose*, then it is
that this demon of humanity seeks *to cast her off*,
and jeopardise her womanhood!—*bastardise her
children !* "

He had been growing taller every sentence   He
had walked close up to the Judge's bench. His eyes

flashed fire His voice, and hands, and arms, and tones, and gestures all grew eloquent. Few actors ever equalled, none could excel it. It was grand!

This was William A. Beach in the Brinkly case, where he won a verdict and a vindication for his client, by $15,000 damages.

BREVITY AS AN ART.

BILLINGS says, " When you strike ile, stop boring many a man has bored klean thru and let the ile run out at the bottom " This alone would be a law lecture, but follow it a moment. What is gained by explaining when the truth is made evident? The ancient king who offered a prisoner his life for answering seven questions was delighted with the beauty and brevity of each answer: " What kind of fish have their eyes nearest together? " was the first, when instantly came the answer, " The smallest "; and so on with the seven. Everything is clearer by brevity if it is clear at all.

Brevity is a fine art in Court. It is a jewel in practice. The interest of a tersely told story is continuous. The late Darwin Hughes was a master of clearness. He had a faculty of making one see his opponent's theory in its weakest light by showing how poorly his positions were matched by the evidence, and how contrary to reason would be an answer to his argument. Some would mistake his earnestness for severity. No one could find him joking during trial hours. Law to him was serious business, an exact science, with very little room for levity, and that never indulged in on duty He would begin with a

witness, if important, with his age, residence, and
business, and pass directly to knowledge of facts and
circumstances, and like husking an ear of corn, in
the presence of the jury, show the ear free from
silk or stalk, and group separate branches of testimony into strong combinations. This is an instance
A rich man had left a strange will, allowing his
children $200 a month, the widow a handsome sum,
and variously disposed of the balance   It was his
purpose to show the mental capacity of the decedent
and the righteousness of the will   He called the
decedent's sister, who detailed, step by step, how he
had acquired his vast fortune, how he managed it;
how the sons were spendthrifts, giving their queer
mental natures, ending with facts to question their
well-balanced judgment—when suddenly one of the
boys drew a revolver and made a pass to shoot the
senior counsel   He was taken in charge safely, and
Mr Hughes remarked in closing, "Nothing could
be clearer that the father regarded his helpless sons
with great tenderness in extending this protection of
an annuity, instead of a fortune, in their evident condition." He rested with this thought and won a
disagreement, amounting to a substantial victory,
for the widow took the lion's share of the rich man's
possessions.

SHARP POINTS OF EVIDENCE.

WITNESSES who argue testimony, and counsel who go over their ground too often, are alike distrusted. It is fair to assume that good evidence needs but little argument even by counsel, and none by witnesses. Men who have fine teams or fine wheat or wool or apples to dispose of, usually let the articles tell their own story.

Arguments are weakening when they are not needed. The more you urge some facts the weaker they seem, but, left alone, like a good joke they would be their own best explanation. Men will not believe impossible or unreasonable things, even if forty witnesses testify to their having happened.

The stopping-place is on the very summit of fact. Let it rest there. Let it require just a little genius to discover it Do not assume that a jury are all sleepers, some are keen-witted and will re-open the case in their jury-room. But if you go over the ground too often, how can they? Halt on the very top of victory, rest with it as a climax.

The cheap wit of playing smart with witnesses and trying to entrap them to please an audience is all lost. Vulgar jokes are utterly useless The bar-room trials are nearly all over, and one who attempts the old-time practices is behind the age, and losing in business. This is the era of *evidence.*

If you have any doubt on this topic, ask any of the panel, after you are defeated, and you will learn that the jury took sides against your client for some pique at counsel or lack of clear evidence. You will do well to consider that the other side may have many

7

friends on the jury, and they will be listened to in the consulting-room. If you have right and justice, and have made it clear, you will be duly credited accordingly.

Over-cross-examination is where very many fail in practice, they want to show off. Of course, if one swears that he saw green grass when the deep snow must have covered it, you can cover him with blushes without effort. If men swear from motive it is well to show it, but the instant it appears let it stand like a house plant in the parlour window—don't meddle with it and kill it.

The average mind will cling to only one opinion at a time, and to fill a jury with abuse of counsel or abuse witnesses is to endanger the verdict. Cases are often measured by counsel if fair or unfair, good or bad, it will show by abuses, or native kindness—the last wins on a jury unawares.

"Other things being equal," says Judge J. B. Moore, of Lapeer—a man of rare tact in a Court room and whose skill won the great Barnard-Curtis murder case at Charlotte, Michigan, by showing that an *ante-mortem* statement of Mrs Curtis was but a *vivid dream* and not a real occurrence—"the man who is clearest and kindest *and most thoroughly* prepared will win oftenest"

Hon. L. D. Norris, of Grand Rapids, Michigan, of State repute as an advocate, adds this terse and striking trial rule, which is full of force and meaning: "Never cross-examine at large! Cases are lost rather by too much than too little cross-examination."

THE STRONGEST REASON.

HUMAN nature responds best to human reason.
What you would have done is what a jury would
have done. "I may be amiss in my feeling," said
Judge Ryan once, in Milwaukee, "but had that
child been a child of mine, this trial would have
never happened. There might have been a trial
for murder! Had that man even so much as
looked his villainy at *my child* and—by heavens I
would brain him as soon as I would a mad dog!
And so would *you*, and *you*, and *you*, and all of
you"; and instantly the jury took sides with the
speaker.

But this was an extreme case, and human nature
was roused at the recital. In all ordinary cases the
strongest reasons are given without passion. Even
in the Ryan matter his highly heated words led to a
disagreement and a final acquittal. Momentary fights
are not the surest in a great contest. Evarts and
O'Conor were always mindful of their effect on the
verdict.

Like begets like, but it must rest beyond removal
by counter-evidence. The counsel who shows his
claim to a jury like Joseph H. Choate does, by lucid
explanation, is surer of their judgment than even one
like his eminent predecessor would be were he living,
not that one is greater than the other, but he is
abreast of the latest methods of dealing with doubtful
cases.

It is useless to expect a jury to share the full
prejudices of both litigants They will divide the
difference. Too great personal appeal may make them

distrustful, too little will endanger your reaching
their best judgment, for *men act best when their
interest is aroused.*

One rule of all should govern an argument. Show
the jury your claim in candour, kindness, earnestness;
show that you believe it; show that you have proven
it, show in statement that you deserve all you ask;
then mould by reason the clay of testimony into the
marble of belief, chisel it to the line of equity,
compare it with justice, and leave it like an undraped
statue.

I cannot better conclude this article than by
quoting rule ten of " Trial Rules " in " Trial Practice "
It cannot be too often repeated · " There is no opportunity better than the earliest. Let the jury know from
the beginning that you believe in your rights and will
fairly enforce them while their minds are as clear as
white paper; *write it on their hearts and engrave it
on their bones.* that your client has the right you
contend for and will ask for none other, but insist
upon justice. On this be so full, so determined, so
fortified with law and reasonable evidence that it will
stand like a rock on a mountain, unshaken by either
quibbles or appeals."

WHAT IS VICTORY?

I REMEMBER hearing a plain man tell a clear truth
once that is impressive from its very simplicity:
" One had better be cheated while young, it don't
cost so much " He said it of his boy's poor trade in
pocket-knives, but it applies just as well in lawsuits.
One had better lose a case early enough to open his

eyes well and avoid such defeat when there is more money in the contest. For this reason, self-reliance will be an excellent exercise in Court practice; one will learn more in a single trial that he wins or loses alone than in many cases with counsel. For proof of this, ask your own experience.

The emergency that brings out latent talent, if a man has it at all, is a powerful means of creating confidence. It will lead him to stand alone, to over come trifles, to demand a verdict, to rely on human nature and oral argument. with good evidence and apt law to win many more victories

The very best victories may be hidden by temporary defeat. The longer litigation may increase your chances and multiply your recovery. If the case has been won on some trifle it will be overturned in a higher Court and win itself, almost, when the supreme Bench is through with it. It is no time to flinch at a small failure. Fifty per cent. of contested trials are tried more than once, and next time it will be the recent loser's turn for victory

Try the early cases alone, try them with energy, try them with warm sympathies; try them with fair means and good evidence; win them without snap judgments; win them without begging a verdict—demand it, be in the right and dare to sustain it; be so reasonable that you can demand it; throw away the trifles; weigh your proof beforehand; see that you are satisfied with it, if not, how dare you hope for victory? The finest law work ever done was the clearest; the best argument is the simplest. The true victory, after all, is the honest verdict of a fairly tried, well-managed contest—one in which neither adversary nor Court nor jury have been fooled, flattered, or overreached, but, when all has been shown as in midday sunlight and the core of the controversy explained, has led to a just judgment. All this is simple, is it? See how it is in actual experience!

TRIAL ELOQUENCE.*

STATEMENT AND CONCLUSION.

JOHN VAN ARMAN's opening and closing words in the second trial of Vanderpool are intensely impressive.

"None of us can understand this case but the one in danger. We cannot rid ourselves of a coolness in the concern of another. But *one* man has felt already the chill and darkness of that dread place to which your verdict, if unfavourable, will consign him.

"A year ago and his condition was as fair as yours. He was not rich, but riches are not needed to be happy. He had his home and the respect of his neighbours, what more could he desire? On a sudden, in the midst of fair prospects, his once quiet town resounds with the wild cry—'Vanderpool has murdered Herbert Field!'

"He was tried, not by a jury, but by the populace. He was hurried to prison. His wife turned from home in the bitterness of desolation, in the depth of despair You have heard the question, Where is Field? If I could, I would gladly call him back from his untimely grave and bid him, with his cold blue lips, reveal this dreadful mystery."

*   *   *   *   *

* Condensed from *Modern Jury Trials*

Conclusion.

"If he is convicted and that conviction is wrong, and some time hence it should be found that, after all, he is innocent, and in consequence of this terrible doom, that you have inflicted upon him, reason should have tottered on her throne, and from being a bright young man in the flower of his usefulness he should become a raving, drivelling idiot, and that wife whose sorrowful face has looked to your eyes for the last four weeks had gone down, heartbroken, to an early grave, it will not be a *twelfth* part of this weight that each of you shall bear, but to *you*, and to *you*, and to each of you will come this crushing weight upon your conscience, in your slumber and in your waking hours, preserved to the day of your death, to upbraid you with a sense of its dreadful wrong! But I solemnly believe when you do your duty, and give him the full benefit of the doubt which these strange circumstances of this mysterious case have left to us all—and I beg of you to do it—you will acquit him! and when you stand for judgment on your own account, the deed will smile by your side, and, like an angel, plead trumpet-tongued for your acquittal and deliverance."

THE EFFECT OF A VERDICT.

It is too often taken for granted that the jury know in advance the limit of a sentence and the degree of a crime. This is a wrong conclusion. Nine-tenths of the average jurymen could not define the meaning of either arson, larceny, robbery, manslaughter or homicide, in terms required by the common law. To such men the best argument is a clear explanation of the crime and its consequences, or, if it be a civil case, the measure of damages.

I think I hear some one say, "Of course, we all know that." But do you practise it? Many things that we know are lost if not put in practice. We could all leap over fences in boyhood, but how many retain their springs through manhood? Men educated late in life, like Lincoln, Schurz, and Giddings, have all their learning at their finger-ends, but jurymen have passed beyond middle age, and may have forgotten first principles

The habit of averaging a verdict is one of daily occurrence One juror will say, "Let's recommend him to the mercy of the Court," and the rest, to be relieved of a dull duty, will consent. The Judge may not have any mercy, and the prisoner's rights are sacrificed. Another says, "The Judge will be light on him—it is a first offence," when the offence is burglary and calls for almost murder's sentence.

In civil cases there may arise the question of "No demand," as in trover and replevin, and this fact, if kept back until after argument, leads the jury to hesitate long on reaching a verdict. I know a case where several hundred dollars in goods hung on a single special question which the jury feared to answer lest it should result adversely, and they disagreed, resulting in a mis-trial and serious loss to plaintiff.

The statement and argument of either civil or criminal cases should begin with the plainest and least-disputed matters. This will more readily secure attention and flatter the judgment of an opponent.

Certainly to concede something is to gain that much of an adversary's confidence, for insomuch as our enemy agrees with us we are not enemies. It is like a heavy load started which moves more easily. With attention and sanction, your reasoning is more patiently followed.

You are sure you have a contest somewhere, but approach it with such gradual firmness that with earnestness and caution you can pass it in confidence. A little hurry at this point may be fatal. Dwell upon it by facts, by figures, by humour, by illustration, by reason, by belief in the positions taken, until you are convinced and feel that a majority are with you in the sensible conclusions of your argument—till you see it in their eyes and faces and every motion of their muscles.

All of the appeals to their sympathy will be use-less, if made without foundation. You will not need to make an appeal unless it grows out of the circumstances that the jury have considered, something that warrants sympathy. If such a time should come, use it but once and then reluctantly; let it grow out of something in sight of the jury or something directly in point that will apply without explaining Men are always ready to reason through incidents, stories, and illustrations that come in the nature of surprises. See that they apply directly, that the jury see the point clearly, then rest.

SKILL IN TRIALS.

THE STORY OF THREE STRANGE TRIALS.

IN the year 1859 two young bankers started business in a small lumber district in Northern Michigan, and succeeded finely for nearly a year. One had experience and $700, the other invested $7,000 and a good social standing. But their qualities did not harmonise, and they dissolved partnership one bright September day and signed articles of settlement, which were witnessed on Sunday at nearly noon.

This bank was a frame building, near the lake, on Main Street. Both were seen to enter alone after settlement, but only one was ever seen alive again. The first thing that attracted suspicion was the absence of the younger and richer partner, whose natural disposition was to hunt and roam about, and but little was at first noted. The older partner was early in the bank on Monday burning some clothing and most of the carpet, and scrubbed out a bloody substance at the rear door. Blood was seen on the back steps leading to the water When questioned, the senior partner gave a poor account of himself, and was arrested. Excitement ran high; and *once*, men wanted to lynch him for murder.

He was held in gaol, and while there made many cross-statements. He pricked a pin-letter, detailing how the murder was committed by two sailors, forged names to it, and attempted to mail it by his wife's aid, who remained in the gaol near him during his detention. This was the most damaging evidence against him—even more than the bloodstains and burned carpet, which told suspicious stories of foul play and attempted concealment. The bloodstains were explained as from nose-bleed. The carpet burning was called a new start—a cleaning-out. The forged entries in the books from $700 to $1,700 were not explained. The concealed coin found in his home was said to be a guard during the delay of trial, the pin-letter to ward off the mob and gain time. All these defences appeared by adroit management on trial, yet he was convicted and sentenced to a life imprisonment.

By an old statute allowing five days in term time, before sentence, to apply for a new trial, he was granted that favour from the fact of his conviction and sentence being on the last day of the term. The fact of so much feeling added another to his accidental victories A change of venue was granted, and able Chicago, Detroit, and Grand Rapids counsel engaged in his defence. These men used the same explanations, and two more. First, by an ingenious time-table they showed how impossible it was to do so many acts—sink the body, carry it to the water, anchor it, have it get twelve miles down the river where found—and be at home nearly every moment of the afternoon and evening, as shown by two witnesses. Powerful arguments followed, and the jury divided nearly half and half.

On the third trial less interest was manifested. The wife's devotion began to tell in favour of her accused husband. A wealthy lumber-dealer furnished counsel and created sentiment by announcing that he had enlisted for life with all his money in the contest. Counsel urged that it was a question of time merely when the real murderers should be unearthed. The bearing of accused seemed harm-

less; two trials had miscarried; Court costs were
increasing; a captain was found who had seen a
half-starved tramp floating in a white boat, with a
large roll of bills, seeking his way to Canada; a white
boat had been seen going down stream on the night
of the murder towards the place where the body was
found with a hatchet-scar on the head corresponding
with a hatchet kept in the bank. The circumstances
grew more and more bewildering, and with superb
tact of counsel were made to tell in defendant's
favour, and, strange to say, he was acquitted! Is
there any greater Court victory of skill in management?

This is the story of the three trials of Vanderpool,
as related by John Van Arman, senior counsel for
the prisoner, who regretted not having had the first
chance to frame the theory of the defence, but found
the old statute and gained the new trial. On what
a slender thread does human liberty often hang!

TRYING HARD CASES.

Old attorneys suffer very little from failure to win
bad cases. Young men can stand but few failures
The public will find out soon enough whether you
win or lose lawsuits, and rank you accordingly.

Young men are naturally distrusted. A name
for losing cases will be fatal if long continued.
Chief Justice Ryan of Wisconsin—long the peer of
Matt Carpenter—sifted his cases with greatest care
and caution, and, although bold and daring in a Court
room, he was timid about starting a doubtful lawsuit
from his office.

To start well is a half-won victory You cannot afford to enter a race without feeling that your harness and outfit are alike trusty and the bridges you have to cross are reliable. Train conductors and engineers are very mindful of such precautions. Hear them trying the wheels at every station! Mark how they tested and tried the iron cables in the Brooklyn bridge to make sure of their quality!

No man ever laid more stress on this point than Charles O'Conor. His researches were marvellous, his prosecution of the Tweed ring, of the Forest divorce case, were matters of life-and-death struggle as it were; he won them when matched by prejudices and by millions. He was so grounded in right as to command and demand a victory.

General Porter's prosecution of Guitteau was a giant undertaking. Tried by interruptions, beset by every effort to break in on the harmony and connection of his theories, he bore himself like an athlete in an arena with a mad hyena at his back, and a band of wolves all around him.

Law practice is strangely varied from civil to criminal. In the first there is no reason for settlement; in the last there should be no room for contention. The law is a serious method of reaching a conclusion that men are unable, or think they are, to reach without it, but a true lawyer should stand as a wall of adamant between his client and fruitless litigation.

CROSS-EXAMINATION.

Ex-Governor Davis, of St. Paul, sends the following excellent rules:

1. Discount by at least 25 per cent. what your client says he himself will swear to.

2. Do as little cross-examining as possible. Never on cross-examination ask a question when you do not know what the answer must be if the witness is honest, and, if he is a liar, don't ask the question unless you are ready to ruin him with a contradiction by facts in evidence or by other witnesses. I have seen more good cases ruined by cross-examination, by the lawyer who ought to have suppressed his curiosity or vanity, than by any other cause.

3. Never mis-state or overstate testimony to a jury, in summing up You will always be detected by some juror, and he will resent your attempt to " play him for a fool "

ABLE ADVICE.*

From Judge C. I. Walker, of Detroit, to Ann Arbor law students:

"For myself, I am a firm believer and admirer of the common-place. I like common-place things; I revere common-place men; I am instructed by ·common-place thought. I like common-place things because they are most useful, the most needful to our happiness—because they are the most beautiful.

---

* As an authority on these topics no man ranks higher in Ann Arbor University than Judge Walker

"I revere common-place men because they are doing by far the most for the well-being of our common race In almost every department of human effort the great work of the world is being done by ordinary men, and this not merely in the department of physical labour. In teaching, both in the home and in the schools, in the learned professions, in literature, in science, in art, in commerce, in government, in morals, in religion, and wherever else there is a call for earnest labour and noble effort—for the active exercise of the intellectual and moral faculties with which God has endowed us, ordinary men and women are, to a great extent, doing the work upon which the welfare and progress of society depend, and are gaining the rewards of such work, solid and otherwise."

Be Humble.

"It is a noble thing for a man to say to himself: 'I am not at all what I vainly fancied myself, my mark is far, very far, lower than I had thought it had been; I had fancied myself a great genius, but I find myself only a man of decent ability, I had fancied myself a man of great weight in the country, but I find I have very little influence indeed; I had fancied that my stature was six feet four, but I find I am only five feet two; I had fancied that in such competition I never could be beaten, but in truth I have been sadly beaten; I had fancied that my Master had entrusted me with ten talents, but I find I have no more than one But I will accept the humble level which is mine by right, and not try to detract from the standing of men who are cleverer, more eminent, or taller than myself. I will heartily wish them well. . . .'

"In your intercourse with clients act with great caution upon the statements that they themselves make. Sift those statements carefully, cross-examine your clients as to the facts, and be careful to ascertain not only what they deem the facts of their case to be, but what they can *prove* them to be. Some clients are stupid, and some are not disposed to be frank with their own counsel. If opinions are rashly given upon the partial and imperfect statements of clients, it will often be found that, though the opinion upon the facts stated was sound, yet that some fact not stated changes the whole character of the case, and defeats the action or the defence, and the lawyer often bears the responsibility of an error that should rest with the client.

"Let your intercourse with the members of the Bar be marked by the most perfect good faith, professional courtesy, and true self-respect. This is easily said, but not always easily accomplished. You will not always receive such treatment from members of the Bar; and in the heat of the conflicts that take place at the Bar it requires more than ordinary self-control to abstain from that which we may thereafter regret. But it is of the utmost consequence to every lawyer, and especially of every young lawyer, that he obtain the respect, confidence, and goodwill of the profession. The profession must ultimately settle his position at the Bar Their verdict will be final. Few things so undermine a man's position at the Bar as to be guilty of sharp practice with his brethren of the profession. No high-minded man will be guilty of it, and no man can ultimately sustain himself in such a course. When associated with others in the trial of a cause, show your readiness to do your full share of the work. Some lawyers throw the work to be done upon their associates, and seek to share only the fees and the glory.

" The trial of a case of complicated facts in law, at the circuit, is a much severer test of a man's power than the arguing of a case in the Supreme Court. In the latter case there is usually ample time for preparation, patient research, and careful thought, that will enable a man of culture, discipline, and fair legal reading to make a good argument, and do justice to his subject. But at a Nisi Prius trial events follow each other in rapid succession, and a lawyer should have perfect command of every faculty of his mind. He must, with an eagle eye, discover the weak points of his own case and those of his adversary, and skilfully cover the one and expose the other. He must make and meet objections to testimony, entirely unanticipated, and argue them—a trying test of his knowledge of the principles of evidence. He must be prepared for unexpected testimony attacking the strongholds of his case, and his ingenuity is put to the test to parry those attacks and avoid their force, or boldly to meet and overcome them. As the case progresses, and while upon the alert in putting in and meeting the testimony, he must be deciding in his own mind upon what principle of law he must rest his cause, or his defence, and shape his requests to charge.

" Previous preparation and study is of great consequence here, but still the exigencies of the case often compel the lawyer to change his ground. As the testimony comes in piece by piece, in disorderly

8

confusion, he must be revolving in his mind how he is to make the most of the important evidence in his favour, and how adroitly and with what logical skill he can make a fact apparently against him tell directly in his favour, and during all this he should be forming the order of his argument, arranging and filling up its framework. And then immediately upon the close of the evidence, while flushed with the hopes of success or depressed with the expectations of defeat, without time to arrange his thoughts, he is called upon to argue the cause. The Court is to be addressed upon the law, and a particular charge requested The jury are to be addressed upon the facts All this requires intellectual skill and training as well as mere power. And the man who proposes to succeed must give himself up with a hearty enthusiasm to his profession. And he who does that, if possessed of good sense, fair ability, and is content to give his days and nights to toil, may gain honourable distinction at the Bar."

READY LAWYERS.

READY lawyers learn to express plain facts in plain words. They will learn from carpenters about buildings, farmers about farming, merchants about business, and of each class about the facts in the line of their own study.

Plain men have been the best teachers, inventors, reformers, and leaders of great measures. They are the best witnesses, the best jurors, the best lawyers, and even the best Judges.

To be a ready lawyer one will need to have law terms well committed—to know the clear names of civil actions and criminal offences, with the gist of evidence required to sustain each, and the best theory of defence followed by able men in like cases.

The statutes of one's State and the higher Court decisions should be familiar books easily reached and readily referred to on any subject; convenient at hand, forms and good material to make papers, deeds, or contracts.

But office readiness is only half the battle. Five more rules of conduct will prevent errors and surprises: Before trial—

1. Find if the client has a case and see that he *can prove it*; then *start right*, and, if already wrong, stop and start again.

2. Note names and addresses, with facts each witness can swear to, and see that his story is consistent and truthful. Brief his facts pointedly. Do so with all testimony.

3. Make the same brief of law points with the gist of cases and pages, so that on facts and law there will be no confusion.

4. See that some one will bring in witnesses without fail, and in a classified order. Check what is proved as you go, and omit nothing.

5. Brief the statements and heads of argument in such order as will prompt a ready address on your chosen theory. By this precaution you go like a trained general into battle. and will be ready for your adversary.

During trial state facts with clearness, directness, and interest, never with dullness. Present proof with fairness, enforce it by grouping the similar facts together, impress it by candid and earnest argument. Consider that the smartest of smartness is to see the right stopping-place and end on the summit.

Object as little as possible. Depend upon your own evidence rather than expect to make the other side prove your case. Think clear through the trial, and keep up that line till the case is ended. Think of it in advance, in the middle, and until the last step has been taken. In the eyes of a just jury every act has its influence. If you are confused they may well be confounded. If you are clear, their duty is lessened.

FIVE FACTS FOR TRIALS.

1. Brief facts and law in *their order*, in terse pocket form, enough to sustain your case and in shape to take in at a glance during the hurry of a trial.

2. Below your points place all the enemy must do to make *his* case, and watch what he lacks to the very end.

3. Make brief of evidence with names, dates, and facts; that greatly helps in questioning. Stop not until each point is put in proof. Have it done in an orderly manner.

4. See and *drill* witnesses to tell the truth in plain words and not from a roundabout hearsay style. Tell them why hearsay is not evidence, and when it is proper.

5. Make points of your address to the jury in bold hand—headnotes only, for ready work. Watch your exceptions and make ready for the next higher Court, where errors are corrected or legalised. Do this with all the skill your genius and tact can command.

TWENTY-ONE RULES OF PRACTICE.*

Book knowledge of law is like a chest of fine tools in the hands of an unskilled artisan—useful, but unpractical, without experience. Practice in law must be largely learned from contests in Courts. It is the lawyer's trade; the more he has of good practice, the better he will know how to apply his learning.

To have the keen tools and the well-learned trade both at command may make him an accomplished workman. No arbitrary rules of study can be laid down, as few follow the whole field of law, and more adopt some specialty, and read accordingly. From observation, practice, reading, attendance at Courts in different States, and counsel with able attorneys, the following rules, with reasons, are given as aids and suggestions in general practice.

The general rules of practice may be confined to twenty-one, and by careful attention to each, great advantage will be gained over a haphazard method of trials, without any fixed purpose in examination of witnesses or argument to a jury. They may lead to winning five extra cases a year.

Rule I

Study every case by itself, thoroughly, and make a clear brief on both law and evidence.

No musician will undertake to execute new and difficult music before a public audience without knowing what it is, and how it sounds; he will drill

---

* From *Modern Jury Trials.*

on every note until he masters each inflection
Actors rehearse before every play. Horses are
scored, trained, and practised before every race.
Boxers, wrestlers, racers, walkers, and boatmen never
start off-handed. It has been told again and again,
that the best-trained athletes were most likely to win,
why should lawyers be an exception?

A lawyer in Court without a brief is like a captain
at sea without his chart; a driver without a tried
horse, a marksman with an unknown gun. But one
with a well-mastered case is strong in every emergency; indeed his victory is over half-accomplished.

RULE II.

*Know what each witness will swear to, separately and
together.*

It often happens that, in criminal cases and family
quarrels, witnesses are separated after the manner of
the well-known trial of Susannah and the Elders,
given in the Bible, where, on the first hearing, with
witnesses all present, it was shown that Susannah
was guilty, but when all the witnesses were excluded
except the person testifying, two material points
crossed each other; the one Elder swore to an offence
under the olive-tree, and the other one to the same
offence under the mulberry-tree—each on the opposite
side of the garden! Susannah went free, while her
accusers were executed.

Show each witness *the importance of candour*, of
holding to the truth, and talking in a reasonable
manner, with facts and circumstances so woven
together as to secure confidence. I remember an
assault case, where an eye was put out with a poker

made from a shovel-handle. In the doctor's statement of why he knew it was that way (instead of a fall on the zinc platform, as claimed by defendant), he showed that the soot in the wound from the poker appeared like butter cut with a rusty knife, which convinced him, and it convinced the jury, who gave heavy damages to the plaintiff.

Rule III.

Open the case fully before any evidence is in.

Whether the plaintiff or the defendant, the claim should be known, and fastened in the minds of the jury, from the start. If for the plaintiff a careless half-heedless statement is made, little importance will be attached to the suit until it opens itself, as it were, and in such cases juries often take an early prejudice that it requires a great amount of evidence to remove. It is therefore very essential to success that a terse, clear, and forcible opening be made, and one that is comprehensive and interesting to a jury.

Especially is this true in criminal defences, where, by an even start, the jury may carry a favourable impression of facts in the prisoner's favour that will come with double weight if opened early in the trial. Experience shows that little is ever gained by a smothered defence. The people's side is of course well known. The defendant, if brought in fresh from the gaol, comes under a cloud; suspicion is cast upon him by the mere force of circumstances, and many believe prisoners guilty simply because they are under arrest. It is of the utmost importance that not one word of evidence be heard in such cases before a full, earnest, and candid opening is made for the defendant. Courts always permit it, and often encourage it. This style of opening has a double advantage of allowing counsel to tell the worst that is likely to be established against the defendant, with his answer thereto, creating an impression that, even with such damaging circumstances, the prisoner is not guilty. It is not the duty of defending lawyers, however conscientious, to convict their clients; such is the province of a jury, and, if ever so guilty, the counsel for defence does his whole duty to present his client's case in a clear, convincing way, that, with the people's side equally well managed, the jury may reach a decision based on the law and evidence, fully, clearly, and evenly explained. An exception to this general rule will be in cases where the defence is made wholly from the weakness of the plaintiff's evidence, or from cross-examination.

Rule IV.

Be forcible, firm, dignified, and clear.

A jury will not be long in reading between the lines if counsel lacks force and earnestness of manner and an interest in his client. For days and months both parties to the suit may have carried their legal trouble at home and at work, like a leaden load, dreamed of it nights, and pondered over it hours together, until their heads would ache with anxiety. To such, a tame or wavering presentation of their side of a suit is more than human nature can endure, and is sure to lose a client, if not the case on trial.

A firm and dignified bearing will be impressive alike to Court and jury, and add respect for your argument that never comes of "shilly-shally" and frivolous statements. The business of lawsuits is to adjust differences, protect the helpless, enforce rights, and punish wrongdoers—it is serious business. But above all, says an old attorney, *be clear*. Many jurors are ignorant of big words; they do not comprehend the real issue to be decided, some understand English imperfectly, others reason in a slow roundabout way, and reach conclusions after a long study and much meditation. Witnesses may be confused by a lack of clearness. It is a good plan to see some experienced juryman, early after a trial, for a few trials at least, and say, How was the case presented? In nine out of ten cases he will say, You ought to have made this or that point a little plainer. The jury did not understand it fully.

Rule V.

Never be bluffed out of Court, but do not begin the bluff.

Once in Court, stay in, and be an opponent, as Shakespeare well describes through Polonius: "Beware of entrance to a quarrel, but being in, bear it that the opposer may beware of thee!"

Some men will fight all the better by being thrown down a pair of stairs, some take to the woods at the first sight of the battle. Clients, suitors, juries, and spectators like a man who can stand in an emergency. A sudden turn in a suit—a new point sprung upon the trial—an enemy from the flank, should draw out the resources of an advocate; and happy the man who is equal to such occasions. If equal, he is marked and remembered long afterwards; but to secure this victory one should be very guarded not to begin the assault, for the vanquished assaulter is always doubly defeated and humiliated. Great lawyers seldom stoop to petty advantages.

Rule VI.

Brevity of facts, terseness of statements, tell best.

Only one lawyer, since Rufus Choate, has succeeded by lengthy sentences as an advocate before juries—Mr Evarts—and his happiest efforts are given in less elaborate style than is his usual custom. Men like Colonel Ingersoll, who cut up their statements *in little stars*, are followed with greater interest.

In the jury room, after the Court charge, when twelve men contend for a verdict, will be often heard such little old sayings as, " The labourer is worthy of his hire "; " They don't make thieves out of that kind of men "; " It takes two to make a bargain ", " Who began it? "; " It served him right "; " Put yourself in his place ", " Give him another chance "; " How many men would do differently? "; " No man becomes suddenly vile."   These are not forgotten.

Rule VII.

Never allow yourself to switch off—" Kill the squirrel."

A trite old saying is, " Stick to your text." In a lawsuit many things happen to try one's patience; witty retorts, stingy replies, low personalities, may so engage counsel and jury as to smother and obscure the case. Jurors take sides, and lawyers that grow personal, and enter into outside discussions, will lead a jury in the same direction. The real winner, after all, is one that with singleness of purpose holds to his point, and hugs the issue to the end. *Harper's Weekly* gave an excellent story of a lawyer selecting a clerk, that applies to this point admirably. The lawyer put a notice in an evening paper saying he would pay a small stipend to an active office clerk. The next morning his office was crowded with applicants—all bright, and many suitable. He bade them wait in a room till all should arrive, and then ranged them in a row and said he would tell a story and note the comments of the boys, and judge from that whom he would engage.

"A certain farmer," began the lawyer, "was troubled with a red squirrel that got in through a hole in his barn, and stole his seed-corn; he resolved to kill that squirrel at the first opportunity. Seeing him go in at the hole one noon, he took his shot-gun and fired away; the first shot set the barn on fire."

"Did the barn burn?" said one of the boys

The lawyer, without answer, continued: "And seeing the barn on fire, the farmer seized a pail of water, and ran in to put it out."

"Did he put it out?" said another.

"As he passed inside, the door shut-to, and the barn was soon in full flames. When the hired girl rushed out with more water"—

"Did they all burn up?" said another boy.

The lawyer went on, without answer · "Then the old lady came out, and all was noise and confusion, and everybody was trying to put out the fire."

"Did anyone burn up?" said another.

The lawyer, hardly able to restrain his laughter, said, "There, there, that will do; you have all shown great interest in the story"; but observing one little bright-eyed fellow in deep silence, he said, "Now, my little man, what have you to say?"

The little fellow blushed, grew uneasy, and stammered out, "*I want to know what became of that squirrel!—that's what I want to know.*"

"You will do," said the lawyer; "you are my man; you have not been switched off by a confusion and a barn's burning, and hired girls and water-pails; you have kept your eye on the squirrel."

A whole chapter is given in this story. It is packed full of excellent advice to beginners, with a few good hints to older counsel. In every suit there is, or should be, one squirrel to kill, and no more.

Rule VIII.

Remember, juries do not know all the facts.

Lawyers appreciate the fact that cases come to office in a vague, uncertain way. The half is not told; and even with several calls and explanations, it is difficult for a counsel to understand the facts of a lawsuit. Think, then, how much more it is to show these facts to twelve new listeners, under the narrow rules of evidence, and to enable men unlearned in the law to reach a correct decision. Is it a wonder that juries blunder? Is it not a wonder that they do so well?

An old lawyer once said, after every defeat in Court, "If you could ask the cause, the answer would be, 'Your man had the wrong side, or they didn't understand it.'"

It may be the witnesses are confused—that they do not talk well in their statements. It is better always to win a suit first in the office. Let each witness be carefully examined and cross-examined and re-examined, until they know the effect of a halting, unreasonable, untruthful story, and know how much stronger a *fact* is accompanied by a *circumstance*.

Here is a suit over a broken leg in a wrestle. Six men swear it was a friendly wrestle, but the injured man says: "I'll tell you just how it happened. The most of the men were half-drunk; it was late in the night; I had been sick; I didn't want to wrestle; he had tried me before, he is too strong and big for me; I shied away from him. Then he came up to me again with his thumbs in his vest, and told me he never meant to hurt me. Just then, as he got in reach, he grabbed me, so (illustrating), and jerked me, threw me against the billiard-table, and broke my leg in two places; I never even clinched with him. Then he bent down and said, almost crying, 'I didn't mean to hurt you Billy; I'll make it all right—I'll pay all it costs you.'" He won, over the six witnesses; he had a fact and an incident. A fact is always stronger and clearer, coupled with a picture of how it happened.

Rule IX.

Show no uneasiness in temporary defeat.

Sometimes a point fails—a branch of a suit falls through. It may not be more than the regiment of an army. It is no time to flinch or show colour; it is a time to bring out mettle. At such times Mr. Lincoln is said to have coolly remarked, "We will give them that point; I reckon they were right there."

Proceed with as much coolness as though the value of
the loss were less than a shilling.   But use the other
forces, and see that the whole bottom of the case
never falls through a small opening.   Good lawyers
say that cases they were sure of winning are often
lost, and others that seemed lost in the middle of a
trial turn out splendidly in the end.   It is well to
have a smooth unbroken line of evidence, but a
sharp stinging defeat on one point, and a pithy
incisive argument on the balance of a suit, may make
a lasting victory.   New trials, frequent reversals,
and discouraging circumstances, may end in a signal
success.

A dry-goods runner was injured in a railroad
accident, and sued the company (Grand Trunk
Railway), and won a $15,000 verdict.   A new trial
was granted, and he gained $26,000.   A change of
venue and one more trial brought him $45,000
damages, which last judgment was *affirmed*.   Nothing
could be clearer than that impediments to a trial. or
set-backs in enforcing a claim, are considered by juries
in the final balance arrived at.   So it is true, when
one contends against odds, juries remember it; and
as sure as any mean little advantage is taken in trial,
so sure the advantage-taker is the loser in the long
run, for juries are human, and human nature likes
fair play in litigation.

RULE X.

Drop a bad witness; Cross-examine only to gain by it.

To cross-examine a sharp witness is to strengthen
his testimony.   Frank Moulton, in the Beecher trial,
was always ahead of his examiner.   To repeat and

repeat often is to weld and rivet with the jury what has been said, as most witnesses would sooner vary the truth than own to a falsehood. It is only on cases of doubtful identity that cross-examination tells so completely, and then it is dangerous ground. To badger a bad witness that, like a racehorse, gains by every break, is no less risky than playing with hot irons where some one will be burned

It is better to seem not to need him, and allow it to go half-noticed, than intensify a weak point on the witness-stand. An exception to the rule is where, in a murder on board a steamer, a positive witness knew just how many officers were on board, who they were, and where they were; but on placing each at a certain point he was confronted by the question, "Who was at the helm?" which so staggered him that he broke down and admitted his blunder.

Another case of identification is where a man called with a forged bill, and took in payment a cheque for a large sum of money. On direct examination he was sure he knew the prisoner to be the guilty party; but being wound up gradually by the dark or light room, whether he had seen the prisoner before, and finally, if he was as sure as though he *actually knew him*, witness faltered, admitted he *possibly* might be mistaken; that he had some doubt, and at last lacked fully enough of certainty to make a reasonable doubt and release the respondent. This cross-examination should be used with caution, discretion, and judgment.

Rule XI.

Make your evidence reach the heart of the case.

Before every trial witnesses should be examined, and never sworn without cause, and held to a strict rule of evidence, until, with truth and candour, they can bring their story to the gist of the action. More witnesses swear around a point, and omit vital and essential elements, than come squarely up to the mark and make their meaning fully known.

Sometimes a case turns on the *intent*, again on the cause, and often on who was the offender. To know what the core of the case is, and hold it in sight, by the proof, is the part of a wise counsellor.

Rule XII.

The main point in law is good evidence

Is an old adage, and one not to be forgotten. Impress both client and witnesses with the fact that a lawyer should know the *good* and *bad* side both, and be prepared to meet either, as scouts are sent out before a battle, so witnesses should be tested before trials.' Show them the real issue, and hold them hard on the line of directness. For, after all, " Man is a mystery that no other man can solve; we are all spirits in prison, making signals that few can understand."

Rule XIII.

Avoid frivolous objections, save your forces for the main chance.

Many a lawyer, to be witty or show off, will talk over and work over his ground in small matters,

that weary the Court, and become stale when needed
in the final argument.

An old lawyer (we quote him often) once said,
"The worst thing that can happen to a young man
is to think he is smart."

Such men grow tricky, captious, and excessively
anxious to *show off* on trials. Juries are sure to count
the cases weak that require such treatment   It is a
mark of vanity to trifle away time on matters that
reach only to the husk or chaff of a case, and obscure
the kernel by such tactics.

Mr. Lincoln was noted for giving away small
points. "We may be wrong on that, your Honour,"
he would say, "I think we were wrong there, but
it is not the gist of the matter, anyway." This fair
play and liberality always told with a jury; and when
he finally said, "Now, this much we may ask, and.
when I shall state it, it will be a reasonable demand "
Then, with all the husk trimmed off, he would state,
in a candid way, such a reasonable request that the
justice of his demand stood alone and relieved of
everything but a fair, just judgment.

Rule XIV

Speak clearly, carefully, and candidly.

Judge Cochrane was one of the most patient and
charitable men that ever graced a Bench. He would
listen a full hour to a dry tedious plea without
turning in his chair. But he sometimes remarked
aside that he knew of lawyers who could talk a full
hour and not make one single point. He believed
many attorneys talked their cases to death. While a
careful explanation is a good argument, a long-drawn-

9

out talk without a definite purpose is likely to lead to the belief that the lawyer is trying to persuade men against their better judgment, and this is sure to react on the speaker.

Jurors respect and admire candour, and occasionally relish wit, as it serves to rest and relax their minds for better efforts; but levity continued at any length is, like a variety show, soon forgotten. The speeches, plays, songs, and sayings that last, and ring in the ears long after they are uttered, that move the judgment and mould the actions of men, have a sacred tinge, often reaching to the fireside, the home, and the tender relations of life. Courts and juries should be impressed with the single thought that you are not inviting them to either a quarrel or a play, but to determine some right and redress some wrong that you failed to settle otherwise. Aaron Burr's great rule was: *Be terse.* The art of selection, he said, was the greatest human faculty. His arguments were made in half-hours, never longer.

Rule XV.

Drop all examinations and arguments in the right place.

When a witness has reached a clear point and a smile follows, perforce, leave the point—let it stand like a rock on the mountain-side, uncovered and alone. To stop short will attract attention and rivet the mind to its importance.

All men magnify discoveries, and to leave it as though a keen-sighted man could just see it, and no more, gives him credit for discernment and relieves his mind of the burden and rubbish that he dislikes to carry.

It is only here and there, like mile-posts, that salient points are fixed in the minds of a jury, and each should stand alone in its strength and clearness

It is the pith of a story to end well. The cream of a joke is in the little things suggested, half-discovered, that leads to new-born pleasure.   A surprise in evidence should end where the story ends, in a climax that rings like a whip-cracker. The same may be said of argument. There is nothing like knowing when to stop. I remember, in a trial where a son and father were parties, at the close of a pathetic paragraph counsel said. " This should not be. Nearing, as we are, the great holidays when children gather round the fireside and tell over the stories of the past, eat and drink and be merry, in the sweet memory of the long ago when they talk of the absent and the loved and lost, this should not be—" And suddenly the father rose up, and, with an emotion that no one could mistake, pointed to the Judge and said " Tell the jury to give him all he asks. Stop; say no more! " and counsel, though only a quarter through, was shrewd enough to stop at a winning point.

Rule XVI.

Let Judge and jury know you mean what you say.

From the date of receiving a case it should grow on the mind continually. By frequent reviews before the trial, by making additions to briefs, and by earnest study, it should be a case for a near friend, which to lose will cause you pain. Let it be as though you might never have another case, and on this one hung all your reputation as an attorney for life. So charge yourself with it that it will come

from every muscle, every gesture, every word, as
deeply in earnest. There is no power in persuasion
like where one believes what he says, where it breaks
down all opposition, and cuts to the hearts of the
hearers like the language of a Moody or a Luther.
Great men have been earnest men. Great orators
have been moved by their own words and arguments,
till they filled their hearers with the fire of enthusiasm.
The earnest words of an old Indian chief will better
express this thought. Before entering a battle he
would call his braves around him, and, smiting his
brawny hand upon his manly breast, would say, " I
know that I shall win this battle · I feel that I shall
win this battle; *it is burning in my body that I shall
win this battle !* "

Rule XVII.

*Consider your adversary powerful, and be ready for
him.*

It was a rule of Napoleon never to underrate an
enemy. In Court trial the enemy is usually, and
almost always, stronger than we expect Hearing one
side, and that imperfectly, and generally well coloured,
the attorney is often surprised to find he has much
to contend with before unknown , and if he has gone
to trial weak in law or evidence, he may find too
late that his enemy is all-powerful and cunning, and
he may fight against odds when he looked for an
easy victory. An easy victory in law is not common;
usually both sides have some rights. Each party is
fortified, or he would have surrendered at discretion.
He may come supported by able counsel, he may
have practised until, like David with his sling,

he can hit his adversary in an unarmed place.
There is only one way to be tolerably sure of winning,
and that is to be always ready, always prepared,
and always willing to provide the best weapons of
warfare.

Rule XVIII.

*Suits turn on evidence of facts, with the application of
the law.*

To make a legal defence, or a lawful demand, the
evidence must be within the rules of law and the
Statute of Limitations

An oral agreement to sell real property or assume
the debt of another is of course void, and the first
consideration will be, Is the demand a legal one?—and
second, Can it be sustained by evidence? It is not
only humiliating, but a source of actual loss in business, to bring a stale suit and find it barred by the
statute, or a good cause and lack evidence. So that,
before going to Court, every case should be tried in
the attorney's office—tried with the evidence and
law at hand, and tried with a full knowledge of the
facts; but more than all, in starting a suit, to use the
right parties, to bring the right action, is vital to the
life of litigation, and no rule of practice should be
more carefully heeded than this: *Be sure you are
right!* If upon the wrong road, the further you go
the more time is lost, and the further you are from
the object to be attained. In a certain suit, brought
within a few days of "outlawing," the plaintiff
neglected an important point in joining the proper
defendants. He submitted to a nonsuit. This barred
the claim, as the adjourned day placed it over six
years past due, while the nonsuit was as though no

proceedings had been commenced. The true temper
of the steel depends alike on the degree of heat and
the correct time to cool the metal; the law and the
facts must be well united to make a judgment
possible.

Rule XIX.

*Twenty questions of fact to one of law will arise in
Court trials.*

· It is seldom that cases are lost on technicalities,
more frequently on defective proof of facts. There
are so many means of negligence, so many releases,
or receipts and discharges, that lawyers are often
defeated by some paper carelessly signed without con-
sulting counsel. In view of these facts suitors should
be cautioned early in the case to leave all settlements
entirely with their counsel and never settle without
advice. There is nothing more annoying to an
attorney than an error that takes his case out of Court
at the wrong time, without securing the fruits of his
labour, and to prevent this he should instruct his
client to keep faith with him and reveal all matters
in confidence, good or bad, and conceal nothing in
the case essential to be known. The more thoroughly
the facts are prepared and studied, the more certain
will be the result. If a case fails by a law-point that
no one can see or prevent, counsel should never be
blamed for it. But a failure on a point of fact that
could be foreseen is an act not often forgiven.

RULE XX.

See that you do your work well.

It brings business. To give one rule for increasing business, embodied in two words, I would say, *Be thorough.* A well-made deed, abstract, or paper, will bring other like work to an office. A well-tried case, fully and forcibly put, will bring other suits. "That is the way," said a listener, "that I would like my suit tried if I had one." He is a worker, is a recommend for a lawyer; he makes his client's case his own, is better, *he wins his cases, is still better!* But no one can win cases without work. Great efforts are made after long study. Judge Comstock worked seven weeks in the Tweed case, citing over five hundred authorities, and, when he reached the end of his brief, saying to the Court of Appeals, "And from all these cases but one conclusion can be reached, and that is, that every man charged with an offence against the law is entitled by the Constitution to a fair and impartial trial by jury for each offence, to the right of challenge, the right of counsel, and to be confronted by witnesses in every case, but in this case it was sought to annul these rules, and by conviction on one offence, multiply it by fifty-five, and imprison the respondent beyond the term of his natural life, and having suffered more than one sentence already, we conclude *he has paid the penalty, he has suffered long and patiently,* and should be released and set free!" The Court sustained this view, but other suits followed.

Rule XXI.

Hold on hard to the strong points of law and facts.

It is related of Lincoln that he seemed utterly regardless of little points, holding to the core of his case, and winning by his liberality and fairness. In the trial of disputed bills he would waive interest or forgo trifles, from time to time, until the close, when he would bend to his work of winning the main issue with a determination seldom witnessed, and, having won the jury by good humour, he would fasten their judgment on the sum he demanded. The higher one rises at the Bar, the less is known of little quibbling demands and defences. In the "upper storeys" men battle for principles and property with manly weapons, as will be seen by the efforts of Stanley Matthews, Gen. Butler, Arnold, Hendricks, Carpenter, and Judge Chipman, and many others referred to throughout this volume.

If there is one maxim more to be remembered than others, in practice, it is, "BE THOROUGH." Is it a demand to collect?—Get it admitted; get it secured; never higgle over trifles; watch the main chance. Is it a compromise between neighbours?—Reach a just settlement, and insist upon it. Is it a family difference?—End the litigation. Is it the liberty of a man in chains?—Show him to the jury in his noblest manhood—surround him in Court with his friends and neighbours, tell what is good of him; assume not that he is wholly innocent, but that he may *not have been proven guilty.* The sacred calling of a lawyer imposes earnestness of manner, study and ingenuity, tact and energy, and a heart full of love and loyalty for right, and with them *every promise should be kept as inviolate as made under a solemn oath.* 'Tis said, " The accusing spirit that flew up to Heaven's Chancery with the *first oath* blushed as he gave it in, and the recording angel, as he wrote it down, dropped a tear upon the word, and blotted it out forever." Why should a brother bind a brother with an oath?

SELECTING A JURY.

To exclude *two* jurymen, without cause, in civil suits, and *thirty* in murder cases and high crimes, is a work of more importance than any one act of the trial—not even excepting the argument.

Men are all human. They carry their prejudices to church, to mill, and to Court, as much as they carry their arms and hands with them. Some are hardened by unbelief in human nature; some are crippled, disordered, and impatient, some are lifeless, and with all the milk of human kindness lacking in their nature, some are noble, generous, humane, and open-hearted, some with reason, others are set and determined. Lawyers should prefer reasonable, merciful, enjoyable, liberal, intelligent jurymen, absolutely free from bias or distrust. It is generally known that ex-policemen, ex-sheriffs, and ex-Justices, with other like ex-officials, have imbibed a deep-seated prejudice for the plaintiffs whom they have served so long, while labouring men prefer their kind, and each nationality will in some degree stand together. So in criminal defences and civil suits these points should be always remembered.

But, presuming the Justices, policemen, sheriffs, and deputies are excluded, and only the honest

twelve remain, who of them are to be chosen? Why,
look at them! Mark their candour, age, humour,
intelligence, social standing, occupation, and let your
eyes choose the most friendly, liberal, and noble faces
—young or old, but better young than old; better
warm than cold faces; better builders than salesmen;
better farmers than inventors, better good liberal
dealers than all. Avoid doctors, lawyers, pettifoggers.
There is a little man, deformed, narrow, selfish,
opinionated. Yonder is a captious, caustic, witty man,
of stale jokes and street-corner arguments; and further
on is a *hard* man, grim-faced and cold grey look,
white blood and glassy eyes. Rule them all off, if
possible. The world has used them ill. They will
spread their misery for company's sake. If you
have been wise, you have looked ahead, read your
directory, and known the occupation of each. All
this is easily done. Jurymen are usually well-known
men, distinguished for wit, humour, wealth, or
business dealings. Chronic hangers-on, unless clear-
headed, can easily be excluded

I have known a sailor on a jury to acquit a sailor
charged with crime. He was clear on the case. A
wrestler once turned a suit for the plaintiff by showing
the jury how it was done, he was *one of them*. In
a robbery case, defendant gave evidence to show that
he won the money at *draw poker*. A keen juryman,
who understood the game, plied complainant with
questions, and drew out that he liked poker—went
to the defendant's room and played, and remarked,
" I am beaten at my own game "; and although the
amount won was over eight hundred dollars in bills,
a gold watch, revolver, and a twenty-dollar gold piece,
the poker-playing juryman convinced the rest that the

exciting game, and not the offence charged, was a clear solution of the so-called robbery

Many a builder or expert has changed the whole twelve by knowing the case. Too much could not be said about the wise selection of jurors.

THE LUCK OF LAW.

To the student at law, and to many men outside of the profession, an *ideal* lawyer is a great orator.

In the days of Webster and Choate, or the earlier ages of history, such a character was worshipped almost as a hero. But learning and the Press, the power of print and the greater development of mankind as a mass, have very much weakened the influence of eloquence.

Within the last dozen years it has become more clearly apparent that evidence, and not eloquence, prevails; and he that has weighed most carefully the history of cases for the last half-century will bear witness that more than one case is decided by the overpowering sentiment of communities outside of either eloquence or evidence.

To be a little more explicit, the *science of success* in the department of law is rapidly changing to business principles. An active, energetic, thorough, and determined lawyer will succeed in his business very largely in proportion to the capital he employs and the energy he expends in his calling.

The term "capital," in law practice, relates as much to character and cultivated judgment of men and things as to any other degree of legal attainment. Indeed, it is the business lawyer with a common-sense view of general subjects, and not the stickler on trifles, that makes his mark in the Courts and in the world. He who will trust cases to men should study the character he confides in.

In the majority of cases twenty times as many questions of fact as of law will arise, and he that is most thorough in facts will be most likely· to win. This, then, is the secret of the whole matter. Earnest attention to details, thorough arrangement of evidence, coolness and absence of anger and excitement, brevity and clearness of argument, honesty and fairness of statement, firmness and decision of judgment, a reliance on reason rather than the biased opinion of your over-zealous client, and deliberate determination to do right.

Eloquence should never be forgotten; there are subjects in themselves eloquent. It is not in words, but in the man, and of the man and from the man, and at the occasion, that eloquence is born. It is never premeditated, but born of the theme and in the counsel But oratory is studied, mastered, and held in readiness for rare occasions.

As nothing should be done to discourage an eloquent appeal, so nothing need be said to imbue attorneys with an over-value of or reliance upon it to win in a lawsuit. The best advocates and orators are well stocked with apt quotations in prose and verse, and add force to their reasons by happy thoughts of other men ingeniously interwoven in argument. On great occasions and in great cases the subject itself may furnish all the eloquence demanded.

In a celebrated case in Indiana a statesman was pitted against a country attorney, whom all expected to be beaten. if not annihilated. The case proceeded.

The country boy was quiet, but clear and determined. He made his modest opening, and waited for the thunder of the orator; but it was like a lion tamed by kind usage; the strength of the statesman lacked a forum for display. He forced his plea upon the jury and they shed tears. He urged his client's cause in all general ways, and just enough to heat his little opponent to a speaking-point. The country boy stood up, stammered (purposely, I have since thought) and stumbled a little, but, clearing his boat from the shore, he launched off and out smoothly, through the long conflicting proof, picking up every point, commenting on it in the keenest, closest style, building such a fire of the little sticks and floodwood gathered by the way that by the light of a blazing sun at midday none could see the murderer and his victim plainer than by the boy's description of the tragic scene. The tragedy was re-cast, the fire and fervour of a boy's warm heart was blazing in every character, speaking from his eyes and hands and face. The jury forgot the statesman, forgot the defence, forgot all but the ghastly deed, held up in such an artful, unerring, vivid manner, that a shudder ran round and round the Court-room by every new discovery. He sank exhausted, and conviction followed.

It was a flash of lightning from a cloudless sky, but the boy had remembered his case—had dreamed it out, thought it over, studied it, kept his proof like a polished knife, and pushed it to the hearts of the jury unawares. It was another David with his little sling and five smooth stones, striking where no armour had been made.

And this is the luck of law. The *luck is work*: the luck is tact; the luck is ingenuity, the luck is in bringing law to a Court with wisdom, discretion, power and logic, tact and genius, well combined, and bringing facts to a jury in the clearest, plainest, simplest possible light, to convince and decide for your client's cause. It will not do to *guess*; he must work—I repeat it, he *must work to win!*

IN THE SUPREME COURT.

Ex-Chief Justice Graves, of Michigan, writes ·

Let every person assuming to be a lawyer consider it his duty to do his best to understand the law, and as a minister of justice to make his office subservient to its rightful administration It is only through the triumph of justice that the highest professional success can be attained. To conquer in a bad cause may procure temporary applause, but the final verdict of the future will reject the glory of the hour and insist upon truth and justice.

The precept of day by day prudence in the Supreme Court may be comprehended by a few general terms.

We may suppose counsel to have the requisite learning. The next thing is to master the particular case, see that the record is correct, anticipate the arguments on the opposite side and prepare to make the best answer admissible, be true and just to your own intelligence and honour, but do not forget that arguments and views which are not quite forcible to you may appear cogent to the Court.

Avoid verbosity, and remember that the members of the Court may be supposed to know many things even among the ordinary doctrines of the law.

Use as much brevity as is compatible with clearness, and stop when you get through.

The question of winning cases concerns both sides, and even in the Supreme Court it is a rare thing for both to succeed in the same case, although it is not so very unusual for the event to disclose that both have lost   The difference between attack and defence prescribes a difference between attacking and defending, and one of the first things for counsel is to' recognise this destination and apply its direct and collateral suggestions to the particular case.   He will not be inclined by choice to help his adversary (a thing oftener done, by the way, than is commonly imagined), and will therefore see to it that he does not entangle himself with incongruities, but confine himself to the genuine requirements of his own side   Except so far as needful to answer his antagonist's arguments, he will rest his case on a few propositions, generally not to exceed three, and on these he will spend the weight of his fire.

If unable to succeed by such means, he would not be likely to do so by expending the same force over a larger ground.   If a battery fire concentrated on a single point cannot force a breach, it would not do better certainly if scattered over a hundred yards

TO BEGIN LAW PRACTICE.

BEGIN law in any State or city with a sense of eternal rectitude: advise every client as you would an own brother.   Be in dead earnest about it.

Consider how completely you hold your client's interest in your hands, and how much depends on your honest judgment.   Use wise discretion.

The law is not a mere scramble for bread-money, for we are charged with the safety of property and the progress of society. Live for some object.

Life is a little journey, where we all hurry and many are injured and impatient, while we are called to set them right under trying conditions. Do so bravely.

The world will measure us by the way we do our duty, as it measures the reaper, the racer, the railway, and the telephone. We must do something useful, real, and of benefit, that shall better our race, and by it we shall be known to have lived once and to have made the world better by it.

LAWSUITS LOST AND WON.

A LAWSUIT is lost or won in many ways. It is won by a clear statement to a fair jury, with enough testimony to convince plain men of your theory, which, with the evidence to match, should be known to counsel in advance of the trial. It is lost by not knowing the enemy's position in season.

Your own client begins the blunder by keeping back part of the facts that will injure him and aid the enemy — facts that wise counsel could easily explain if advised of earlier It is often lost by a wrong theory—one taken to please a client, when he has no right to dictate more than to suggest facts, and let counsel prescribe remedies.

These over-wise clients, that come so near being lawyers and always blunder in their plans, are dangerous advisers! Suits are won very often by the skill of advocates, or tact in the use of evidence. It is a sort of legal workmanship—a sending the shot to the centre of the target, instead of out among the leaves at random.

The science of good practice is that art which teaches a builder to discard bad timber, to prepare what he uses with precise care, and fitted with precision to the members of the building, that teaches a mason to make joints before reaching the building he is erecting.

The plan in the brain is the science of it all. The skilled architect builds for eternity; the sham tenant-house builder uses rubbish in his foundations. Suits are lost by a lack of interest in details, a lack of clearness in evidence, or some want of tact in the conduct of counsel.

TO YOUNG LAWYERS.

A LEADING daily paper answers a young farmer-boy who would be a lawyer, and gives him several points by which he may succeed, condensed as follows " 1. Be one who is selected counsel for a corporation. 2. Make a hit in some big criminal case. 3 No one can dispute but unscrupulous lawyers make the most money. 4. Let one once secure the reputation of knowing how to handle a jury, or 'stand in' with the Judge, or break a witness all up, and he is certain of a large income."

What a mess of pernicious nonsense! No lawyer ever wrote it! It lacks sense, judgment, and decency! It is positively vile—a libel on Courts and lawyers, and is basely unjust and unreasonable. Such has not

10

been even the lowest public estimate for years, to say
nothing of a fair opinion   To be a corporation lawyer, says Col. Van Arman, is a dire misfortune to a
beginner, for it shelves him forever.   He must be
the loser in very many cases.   He will run in a rut,
and soon become a mere money-maker, which is a
trade by itself, and a side-consideration to men who
would rank very high in a profession early in life.
A lucky hit in a criminal case and the unscrupulous
lawyer come next in order.   Lawyers of neither
class are to-day leaders of the Bar, and this is
especially true of the latter.   The lucky hit does not
come by accident   It is a matter of keen insight,
correct theory, and careful preparation; the genius
of taking pains to go to the place of shooting, to
visit the scene of the tragedy, to fill one's self so full
of a case that it bubbles out at every pore, with the
law at hand and evidence to match the theory.   Good
evidence is about the best luck any lawyer ever yet
heard of.   There is no such thing as "handling a
jury" for many cases together, without the essentials
just mentioned.   Juries are convinced by arguments
on evidence, and a lawyer who claims to "stand in"
with the Judge is a rascal that any Court will repel
as soon as he knows of such an impostor.   The best
"standing in" is to get the case ready in the law and
facts, and be honest about it   And as for breaking
up witnesses, the hired girl's remark, "*And what
would I be doing all that time?*" applies aptly   From
fifteen years of reading and saving odd cases, most
of them read six times, to make books of, and quite
a large number of visits with men of rank in law,
like Matthews, Beach, Curtis, Porter, Van Arman,

Dougherty, and their class, I have learned to distrust in every sense unscrupulous methods. They bring a bitter sting sooner or later, and of all dangers to young lawyers the risk of trying to break up a witness is most hazardous, for *what will he be doing all that time?* Killing your case by inches; saying hard things; intensifying bad testimony. I could say more, but you are lawyers and can see it easily. The richest and best lawyers have a reputation for skill, honesty, and integrity, and often for eloquence. The greatest are upright, honest *men!*

COUNTRY LAWYERS

A city physician has many advantages by his large circle of acquaintance and social connection over one born in the country, but a city lawyer can never claim such preference. The former will meet a larger practice as the wives and children of the rich in cities more often call a doctor, while the poor make their own medicine With a lawyer the case is reversed The rich men of large cities have their counsel hired by the year, and no matter how large their business, no young man can expect to control it until he has become established, not only as a graduate, but as a faithful and skilful man in special cases. He must either win or be counted a failure in Court cases. A poor young lawyer in a city has but one dream of preferment—he must win and win often The city friend will have his diversions—dances and parties, with a thousand and one means of enjoyment. The country lawyer in town will ignore most of them and rely on his Court victories for distinction. From the first case to the last he throws his soul into the contest—dreams of it, thinks of it, reasons of it when alone, goes to Court brim full of it, speaks of it so earnestly that, like the tongues of dying men, it compels attention by deep harmony. Country lawyers have long been known as industrious When they move to the city, as did Gordon, Brown, Hendricks, and McDonald of Indiana; Van Arman, Swett, and Lincoln of Illinois; Beach, Shaffer, and Pryor of New York, or Butler of Massachusetts—they carry their courage into Court, imbedded and coined in their very being, through a life of early hardship, with one long line of contest, beyond the reach of easy access to many books, they commit all the more thoroughly the principles of common law and evidence, and mass their forces in solid columns Wealthy lawyers are of all men the most hindered and delayed in starting, by the very reason of their riches. They will spurn the smaller Courts and wait for respectable practice, which comes only to such as are ready to do it successfully and never as an experiment; and of all men best drilled in general practice the village lawyers on the inland county seats are the most ready, most apt, and most earnest, and win their cases the oftenest.

HABIT IN COURT.

THE force of habit is more powerful than law or reason. Once fully formed, it controls the greatest as fully as the humblest, undermining the strongest mental and physical qualities, destroying the purest characters, changing the noblest natures.

I have in mind three instances· One a shrewd,
well-read, ingenious lawyer who gradually drifted into
a captious, tricky practice, secured some fame by it,
won a few nonsuits and demurrers, took in a few
ten-dollar notes, and failed to win on the merits, until
his present practice is but trifling

Another is of one presumably witty, harsh and
sarcastic, abusive if he ever can be, overbearing if it
suits his purpose, caring only for self, and daily
losing the good will of his brother lawyers. He
assumes to be successful, but is a positive failure in
all that is noble, manly, and sincere to his equals or
superiors. I think it is clearly the force of habit that
is undermining his usefulness.

A third one began by modest charges and respectful bearing toward others; gained in esteem by fairness and kindness; acquired friends even among his
opponents, became trusted for his integrity, held
the good opinion of the Bar and of his clients; was·
promoted so often that many honours have been
declined by him, and now, in ripe age, is turning his
eyes toward sunset with a face unmarked by harsh-
ness, and will ere long, go over to the majority,
mourned and remembered for his goodness as well as
greatness. Shall I draw any inference, or am I not
clearer without it?

THE REWARD OF VICTORY.

A YOUNG lawyer's beginning is like a racer without
a record, like a patent in its model state—he may
be useful and *may* prove a failure. Somebody must
experiment with him, for he lacks development. If

he runs without friction and does the work of experienced counsel, his pay will be less than a tenth of
that allowed the senior, and the credit will still belong
to another.   If he fails—a thing he dare not do,
and must consider impossible—it is charged to his
lack of tact or genius, when in fact he may even be
much brighter at his age than Webster would have
been with like experience and training.   But fine lines
are not drawn in such cases.   He must *win*, and that
settles it   Neither his rank in college or standing
at home will replace the one thing he is hired to do
—to win suits   Friends may gather him an audience,
smiles and kind faces may welcome his coming,
but cheers are out of order in Court rooms, and in
the supreme moment of a young lawyer's peril, the
simple question over all others will be. Is he ready
with his evidence? Is he ready in his mind? Is he
equal to his case?   Has he learned it carefully?   Does
he know his ground well?   Can he win?   The reaper
that binds best, the racer that runs best, the machinery
that works best, the actor that draws best, the
doctor that cures best, and the lawyer that wins
oftenest, will be paid most liberally.   The test is a
severe one, an unfair one, and many a boy lawyer
has failed under it who should have succeeded, while
many a one wins, not by knowing how, but by an
Herculean exertion   The courage of victory is a
reward beyond all retainers.   The merit of success
is the lawyer's best paymaster, like the Roman
soldiers who had been victors in battle, their eyes and
their arms proclaimed it.   So the sequel to victory is
success in anything.

LAWYERS' FEES.

IT is said that several New York lawyers, like Curtis, Conkling, Evarts, Pryor, and their class, could very easily accept silent retainers by the month or year, and remain away from Court contests entirely, while they enjoyed a princely income, but prefer the excitement of advocacy to the duller work of mere money making

It is well known in cities that the highest chargers in law practice are not the best lawyers, but often men whom others engage for some special gift or influence—generally the knack of gaining an early victory. The hardest workers and most conscientious men in practice are more of the Edmunds, Thurman, and McDonald stripe, who have no time to make money, and satisfy their conscience with smaller charges: either of these men could easily grow rich by higher charging.

More than likely the average lawyer can recall many men in practice whose gift in gaining cases was far superior to that of saving silver. Webster and Choate, Carpenter and Beach, Storrs and Lincoln were all poor, or not rich, advocates. and yet with talent of the highest order, while hundreds of others, inferior in genius, learning, or character, have lived in luxury and died in splendour (if owning money is splendour) from some strange gift of grasping riches.

To sum it up briefly there is but one conclusion to the whole matter, and that is the little lawyer, within the larger one, prompts the other into making low or high charges, and in proportion as the little inside man (sometimes called the soul) is large and influential with the outer counsel, will be the measure of the fees demanded. The great and generous, the strong and noble, can afford to be reasonable · to them victory is recompense, and an honourable victory is a rich reward, while the narrow and selfish must have money or they lose all enjoyment in law practice. Lawyers like others weigh with strange balances.

A VEST POCKET BRIEF.

MONDAY.—The past year was one of progress, but it might have been better. Yes, there was a suit nearly lost for lack of a little clearer evidence. We will see that does not happen this year.

Tuesday.—A juror mentioned it, and of all men to learn practice of, a juryman is one of the best and safest. We will keep a sharper eye on absolute clearness of evidence—that which seemed clear to our client was vague to the jury. It is not an easy task to convince twelve men on either side of any case.

Wednesday.—The brother that interrupted an argument and got a stinging reply will remember it and pay it back some day; even we will not forget it. An injury resented leaves a sting to heal slowly, it may take years in curing, while the satisfaction lasted but a moment. It will be better to omit that practice this year.

Thursday.—The man with a "genius for blundering," as one termed it. Well, what if he had?—he was young and impulsive; it would have been nicer not to have noticed it; the poor fellow will carry that sentence to the Court of memory, and hold it like an appeal case in Chancery, and decide it against us often when alone Nothing of that sort shall happen again, the year must run with less friction.

Friday.—A half-dozen clients called at busy hours and went away early. They made their cases very plausible, for their side, and omitted all mention of their adversaries' position; by ignoring this evidence we were taken by surprise and nearly lost the contest. We will study the other side this year. The *other* side is the one that is not so easy to win over.

Saturday.—What is this law business anyway, but an endless quarrel for somebody? The more some quarrel, the more they like it. The best way to hush up a personal contest gracefully is to make the angry one pay for it at the time—to fix the fees liberally at the earliest beginning They like lawyers best then, we will try it this year as an experiment.

Sunday.—The best rule for the year, in a nutshell, is this · select cases with an eye to certainty; prepare them with a view to clearness, end them at a point of the least loss to client and the most margin to counsel, always believing that a certain fifty is better than a doubtful hundred, while the gain of money by the loss of friendship is a poor investment.

THE BEST LAWYERS.

I HAVE noticed various items of interest in recent exchanges on this theme, but in none is the theory carried out to a complete conclusion. It is a common thing to speak of a lawyer as "a first-class lawyer," or "a rising young lawyer," or "a third-rate lawyer" —the last title is given by the fellow who has just been defeated in Court by the "third-rate" advocate. Some have the habit of thinking that only lawyers in large cities like New York, Philadelphia, or Chicago get their full growth and become great lawyers; some assume that advocates cannot of course be learned in the law.

A close reading of history will kill off most of these theories and change one's convictions materially. A lawyer may be entirely first class *of his age* and nature of his business, and age with experience should always enter into the estimate; many a man has never been tested—never been tried But for some singular cases Patrick Henry may have remained without a record, and Abraham Lincoln have died without a bright name as an advocate—neither enjoyed a city practice; and men like Beach, Shaffer, Porter, Vorhees, Waite, Carpenter, and Hendricks all attained fame in reality while country lawyers. They were not born in, but CALLED to city life Some of the best lawyers never reached fame till after death Ryan was one of this class—an unknown man of Wisconsin with a Websterian genius who *knew the law* and how to handle it.

But as was recently said in the *Daily Register*, "to know the law is not enough to make a great lawyer." He must apply it, win by it, bring out results and enforce attention, as did Seward and Webster, Choate and Tom Marshall. Great lawyers are great in genius, and to underrate them when merely advocates is the greatest blunder. What is an advocate but one who can urge his position as did Cicero in the defence of Gavius?—like Graham at the trial of McFarland, Brady in the trial of Sickles, McSweeney in the Gov. Scott case, Curtis in defence of Buford, Crittenden in the Ward trial, and Vorhees pleading for Mary Harris? These are a handful of the advocates who have moved their States and moulded public opinion in trials not by dry law alone—for that is mechanical, that is book-keeping, that is abstract of title work, that is something that money will buy and pay for, but genius, sagacity, power, influence, character, eloquence, and manhood are gifts of greatness inherited from the Almighty, and developed by ripe experience. *Great lawyers must be good advocates.* Good lawyers may be such and not be advocates; but leaders of men and moulders of minds must be more than title searchers, precedent finders, or statute interpreters—they must be men like Webster and Gladstone, who seek out the right and lead other men to believe it and follow it, and *create* laws and govern nations. Great lawyers are greater than law itself.

I WILL.

A QUESTION that troubles young lawyers is where to locate and what branch of practice to select. This puzzle lasts even into middle life with many able men, and some never solve it; life itself is an unsolved riddle.

Letters from Dakota, Oregon, Iowa, Georgia, and Arkansas indicate a fast-growing settlement in each locality, and where growth is rapid young lawyers secure more chances of promotion, while in Eastern and Middle States habits are fixed, titles are established, and older men do the leading business.

But there is a place for everyone of genius and ability somewhere, and only let him say, " *I will reach it,*" and he is half to it already. Men live where their hopes are, and prosper when they *will* prosper. Men invent when they have courage to think out problems alone and advance them The man who surrenders to a theory like this—" I'm only a little moth around the candle of the earth, burning my wings with each flutter, and doomed to fall unknown and early into an unforgotten hereafter "—is very likely to do so : he is half way on the journey.

Men who have within them the " *I will be a lawyer, and a good one,*" the " *I will live happily, battle bravely,*" the " *I will succeed* INWARDLY," must make a bright mark some day, for such lives are never failures, they are heard of, marked, remembered. "Make up your mind to have a front seat in life, and you attract to you the powers that carry you to it."

Confidence in yourself, the " I will " is everything. Look at the leaders of great enterprises! They seem

to care little for competition; most of them are
sharpened by it. They aspire to be first, and the first
is ever just ahead of them. They have already half
reached it when once fairly started. *Think* to the
front and you will get to the front; lag to the rear
and it is ever ready for your coming.

Get out of the notion that the man who cites the
most law and reads the most reports is the best
lawyer. No man carried fewer books to Court than
did Carpenter. but he carried his manhood there,
always, his clear insight was thought out by himself,
and his facts applied to principles and results demanded. It is not the most learning, but the best
wisdom, that wins. What a weak ambition one must
have to spend a lifetime in dreaming over the prospects of personal failure! Why not anticipate success and aim for it? The courage of the " *I will* " *lauyer*
secures him first standing-room, next an opening, and
early a front seat in the ranks of his profession.

If you never have set your heel down with emphasis, in an " I will " determination to win, the sooner
this resolution is reached the nearer you will be the
goal of your ambition. The hand is never stronger
than the heart, and the man is never greater than his
mind. His life is below or above his true condition,
very much as he wills it; and no one will cheer him
till he wins something worthy of applause. The
world is both stingy and liberal, reluctant to risk on
uncertainty and willing to advance thousands on
ventures when successful. The demonstration of
success is what men wait for and demand.

THE ART OF AN ADVOCATE.

YOUNG lawyers often ask the leading question by letters from Maine, Georgia, and even far-off Oregon —"Who is the first living advocate of our day?" To which must be the answer, "No one is first in everything." Webster was, but he is dead.

Measured by the art of statement before evidence and argument, Leonard Swett ranks very high; by the test of winning cases, Judge Curtis of New York is famous; by the power to plan, General Butler of Boston; by the genius to convict, Major Gordon of Indianapolis; by the power of trial eloquence, Senator Vorhees, by poetic oratory, genius, and versatility, Colonel Ingersoll, and yet a hundred others might be named of splendid talents and superior ability.

The marvellous gift of Beach to make men cheer or make women cry, to divide a jury and charm his hearers, or of Carpenter to move men's fancy like a singer's voice, or Lincoln's wit that won away an audience by its force of truth, were separate arts of separate men, and no one man ever had them all. It is not natural that they should.

All men are not alike in size, or build, or voice, or imagery Some are taller—others grander. Some are sharper—others braver. Some are quaint and others deep. Some are touching — others brilliant. Now and then an orator appears with many elements combined. Seward was one; Douglas another, Choate another, and Webster higher than the rest. Webster was grand.

But the theme of advocacy is not as Webster knew it. The rules are changed. Webster under shorthand work would never shine as brilliantly to-day as he did in his day. His powerful diction was of a measured kind. To-day the Press would tell it faster than he could speak. Most sentiment is dead to-day before the orator's part begins. We hear great plays night after night; but trials are like novels—once the plot well known, the deeper interest dies away.

Real advocates, just now, are men whom men *believe, for men do read of men.* The well-read man, the *well-up* man, the head to plan and nerve to execute, will rank according to his gifts, even in the brightest blaze of a printer's light. If you follow the leaders of the Bar to-day, they are well-rounded men in general knowledge, both in and out of books. They may have travelled much, they *must have practised much.*

It is not a theory, but "a condition that confronts us." That condition is the *power* to *plan* and *win cases.* Every client believes in his case. He over-states it. He may lie a little about it. He magnifies his rights oftener than he understates them. If he be a criminal, his soiled character is revealed midway at trial—just when you have no means to meet it. If he be a contractor, he hides the poorness of his work. If a defendant he "*sets off*" too much, and even if a human being has been killed, the truthful story, which may permit an honest motive to be shown in self-defence, is often told too late.

It is clear, then, that to be an advocate to-day requires one great gift, if all others fail—*the gift of getting at the cause of things.* Solomon's wisdom in detecting the real mother of the child, and the real flower, Daniel's art in Susannah-and-the-Elders case, Portia's ruling on the pound of flesh, like Evarts in the Johnson impeachment trial, and Lincoln with his Almanac, are but so many ways of *getting at the cause* —or wisdom at the time that tend to make such counsel great by being equal to the case in hand.

Even Depew's wit is but a quaint telling of the things we already know. So the art of the advocate is in' his way of cutting knots, and telling things so as to be believed—*convincing* men *of the theory he urges*—touching their nature—carrying their reason —showing them the right and leading their conclusions to his own. Success in law and anything is the thing that succeeds To plan well is to win often. To plan ill is to lose always. *Think what a gifted man an advocate must be when liberty and millions hang upon his power.*

Great men are not always wise. But most men are stronger than they know. The lion's jaws let go sometimes when taken by the hands of men. Seized by the tongue with a grip of death, a little New Mexican killed a monster cinnamon bear. He saw and knew just where to place his hand He took his enemy by the tongue—a fine art in law. With any other grip, the bear would quickly be outside the man. It is the *aim* one takes—the vital part he touches—that brings down the game. In law, in life, in business, and in everything, it is the accurate *plan*, the well-directed work, the *genius* to foresee, the striking where no armour is, that wins. Look at the giants in our business world—they all foresee. One may win with sympathy in law—not often, one with eloquence— rarely now, one with wit—an ancient art, one with insight—the latest art of all, but to expect success without keen forecast is unreasonable. The world advances rapidly in science and inventions. It must advance in law. The greatest study I can name to men, is a thorough study of the works of men. Absorb the plans and speeches, arts and works of men, and emulate them with the best grade of your own in every case. *Think to the front* and *grow in that direction.* Use every element that you possess or can command— and use them in right ranges.

TACT IN TRIALS.

1. MAKE a good bargain about your fee for services. Believe only one-half that a client tells you. Let him produce proof of the other half His zeal and self-interest will deceive him Don't let it deceive you beforehand See the witnesses before you plan your case. It will help you to know what the proof is like.

2 Look over the jury list before term day with care. Study their trades and select a young man for the defence, an older one for conviction. It is a wise selection to avoid very old men.

3. Light-haired men are rarely harsh judges Fleshy men are always good-natured. Exclude cynical men—they are hard to convince Warm-blooded men with fair faces are the most humane.

4. Begin the trial in earnest, from the start. A case well started is over half won What you believe clearly is a quarter-pole passed. Whenever you doubt, jurors become doubtful.

5. Study the result, as it *should be* if decided honestly. Never forget the side you are on. Weigh

11

the other side long enough to be a judge of it. See the final outcome before it is too late.

6. Ever be strong with your evidence. Twenty counsel can't win without it   Don't make too much by counting. Three good witnesses are better than ten poor ones. Two are enough on any fact but character   Beware of the *character* of *character* witnesses.

7 Be anxious to win, but never be anxious to show it   A jury studies the method, as well as the manner of counsel   Be neither sharp, tricky, nor too confident—the more you are of either, the surer is your failure   Good cases are won without tricks— evidence wins better.

8. Abuse is not argument, no matter who gives it Assertion is no proof, even if a giant tells it   Loud noise is not evidence. Earnest reasoning convinces men when sent to the heart. The bullet has power by the force that propels it

9. The genius of selection is the rarest tact in trials.   Select your strong points and rightly urge them, select the right proof and give it orderly, select wise counsel and be frank with them, select cases cited that apply to the issue; select the right basis of judgment   The gift of selection is the genius of victory.   To compare what men believe with what you want believed is argument.

10. The best line of argument may not be known in advance.   The contest reveals it in the trial.   It is often made on opponent's errors or evidence.   It may be an exposure of tricks or bribery.   It may be of incident or eloquence—a tact in trial that changed

the verdict. Sense, reason, and equity; wise selection of jury; kind and manner of witnesses and right conduct of counsel' in urging his rights, will win a lawsuit. What is wise with a jury and what is unwise, men differ on—some urge too much; others too little, others never put the right thing in the right way.

Law is a science. A good trial is a fine art.

To win is the object—to lose is the dread. The sting of defeat heals slowly. The flush of victory brings business. The loss of a book account may be the loss of thousands. The loss of a case may ruin a home. The absence of a witness may mean a prison for a lifetime! The power of a story may save a father to his children. The turn of a case is like the wind in winter—we know not its direction save as we feel it What a science—what an art—what test of genius—what a forum for wisdom and eloquence, is a trial for a life before a jury of twelve with a nation for an audience!

Go in and Win

A lawsuit is much like a duel One or the other is wrong to begin it, but which one is wrong takes a long costly suit to find out; either could easily settle it when it begins—either could settle a duel. Neither is disposed to give a little. Both go in to win.

The cost of a suit is never noted in starting. That is the best time to make a bargain about it. Both sides are in earnest, each would win by all means, but only one side will win—in fact both must lose heavily.

The cost of attorneys, the expense of witnesses, the worry of waiting, the anxiety over the result, the loss of time, of rest and ease of conscience, are sure to tell on the suitors before the end comes. Why will they do it then? Why will men quarrel, or bet, or fight a duel?

Assume they will fight and enjoy the luxury of a lawsuit, let them pay for it and make the best of it. The best use of a lawsuit is to convince men they are in error. If they win they are in error They never dreamed it would be so costly, so lengthy, so bitter, so curious.

Long before the trial ends they have caught each other in as many lies as there are shingles on the Court house—they think so, anyway. They never told quite all of their own case to their counsel. They shaded it slightly—kept back a little of it.   There was a confession or a term of imprisonment between them and a good character—yes, and a bunch of letters to give the case away. If the trial is a criminal one, and the question of character is in issue, some such thing often happens They have signed a receipt in full if the claim is important. They have admitted too much of the debt, or broken off a half settlement, or let out the truth in a letter

But no one can guess these little things that hinder and confuse a trial lawyer. "Did you not sell this claim to your counsel?"—"No, sir." "What about this paper?" (A bill of sale filed, assigning it.) "Did you call upon complainant and urge him to settle for $200, only last February?"—"Yes, sir " "Is this your letter?" These are the statements that counsel are surprised by.

By a little more frankness all could have been clearer. A general who met a concealed enemy might expect it more, but would reprimand a picket guard who *knew of an enemy*, and gave no notice of it. Clients are too proud of their case to reveal all the facts that may be proved against them.

They go in to win, and go in recklessly. Their chief reliance is upon their lawyer. He is powerless without proof. A medium lawyer with good evidence can win over the finest counsel without witnesses. One might as well undertake a race with a fine driver without fast horses, or a fast horse and a rickety wagon.

The lawyer *may win* on a law point—but not one time in twenty. The masses know too much of law to be engaged in a contest that has no facts for a foundation. The case must turn on a contract requiring some act to be done that is left undone, or on a duty to use care and caution, or on a lack of some written agreement required by statute.

To go in and win you will need to prepare for it. The first is with means; the next is with proof; the last is with absolute candour. To get the last is the more of all, and yet as much need as either. To this end witnesses should be examined alone. Like an independent singer, any good witness should stand alone. He should be told that in telling the truth no one is ever much puzzled—no one need hesitate. It is always the same story. It must be to be truthful

But one can tell it and *believe* it. He can tell it to make men doubt or make them certain. To win, each main fact should be certain. Who would risk a doubtful gun in a duel? Who would load it with poor powder? Who would fire it without some practice?

If the client does his part, the attorney will do his;
and a good retainer is an important prompter to duty
in a case of importance. Let the pay be made
certain, the proof be made adequate, the facts be
analysed, the witness examined, the vouchers in-
spected, and the guns are in order—even then you
may meet a dangerous jury.

The matter of a jury's selection is a gift of nature.
Lawyers must judge human nature carefully: ex-
criminals are harsh judges—ex-officers are bad for
the defence. Grizzly, hard-faced men, with wilted,
miserly features, are as stupid to talk to as a straw-
stack. They don't even give back the sound to you.
Men under fifty-five—clear eyes, receptive faces. not
too great, or too much above an average—are the
right judges. Sense and reason will reach them, for
they want to do right.

THE LAW OF SELF-DEFENCE.

The lesson of this argument is in the quick turn of
little interruptions, and the making a defence out of
the people's case. The proof of a broken-up home
avenged was shut out, as it happened seven months
before the assault on the commons of Detroit in 1886.
After citing three cases in 38 Mich , counsel was about
to repeat some words of Blackstone and Cicero on the
meaning of self-defence and was thus interrupted:

The Judge "Cicero is not authority."

Mr. D. "True, not in a legal sense, but his words
are the words of wisdom, sanctioned by age, and,
like the citations of Shakespeare, are believed by
mankind for that reason."

The Court: " But you cannot read to the jury from a printed book?"

" No, your Honour," said counsel, " I have no such intention, I can easily recite words from memory; they are better words than my own, and I adopt them

" ' This, then, is a law, O judges; not written but born with us, which we have not learnt, or received by tradition, or read, but which we have sucked in and imbibed from Nature herself, a law which we were not trained in, but which is ingrained in us—namely, that if our life is in danger by robbers or enemies from violence, every means of securing safety is honourable! For laws are silent when arms are raised and do not expect to be waited for when he who waits will suffer an undeserved penalty. Reason has taught this law to learned men, and necessity to barbarians, and custom to all nations, and nature to wild beasts, that they are at all times to repel violence by whatever means they can without deciding that all men may fall by the weapons of their enemies.' "

In the Scott case, Ohio, a father shot one for an injury to his boy. In the Newland case, Indiana, a father shot the seducer of his daughter In the McDonald case, California, and in the McFarland case, New York, the husband avenged an outraged wife and injured home, " AND IN EVERY LIKE CASE," said counsel defiantly, " THE PUNISHMENT HAS BEEN MERITED BY THE SLAIN AND THE COMMUNITY HAS APPLAUDED THE AVENGER'S COURSE, WHILE THE CRIME OF THE AGE HAS BEEN LESSENED." In the great Dilke case in England a distinguished ex-member of Parliament has been driven into exile and disgraced by the verdict of

a jury for a crime of this nature. In a dozen States
of our Union marriage laws will be more respected
when better executed. We want fewer divorces, we
want less outraged families. It needs a few examples
of extreme punishment to enforce attention and create
respect for family rights in America. If this be
balderdash, as stated by the learned prosecutor, give
us more of it!

Self-defence is not a defence of one's person
merely, it is broader, greater, and has more meaning
in it. In the words of Governor Crittenden: "What
is self-defence? Am I to protect my person merely,
to stand by and see my child, my wife, my property,
my helpless ones destroyed or taken, and resent not
the injury? No, no! The law never was so narrow
as that. If I had no greater right than that I'd raise
my own wild hand and take my life and hurl it back
in the face of my Maker as a thankless gift!"

This was said in the Matt Ward case, where Ward
merely defended his little brother from a teacher's
insult, and Ward was acquitted.

The Court interrupting—"You should not com-
ment on outside verdicts not reported from higher
Courts." "Not reported from higher Courts?" said
counsel warmly "I'll tell your Honour why they are
not reported! The best ones are reported in circuit
Courts I have searched the records for two hundred
years, and there is not a case—no, not one, where the
law of self-defence has been used—especially where
one has defended an outraged home—that a jury did
not promptly acquit the defendant. In the words of
the great and gifted Storrs in the Cochran-Hayden
case in Wisconsin in 1880, where Cochran shot Judge

Hayden for an injury to his wife, Storrs said—"You must not tell what counsel said," repeated Judge Swift "Well, then, *I say, laws are not strong enough, statutes are not broad enough, and never will be, to restrain a man's arm from redressing a wrong where his household has been outraged!*"

This is no more than Judge Ryan of Wisconsin uttered in the Booth case, where a young girl was seduced by an editor. Ryan said, "Had that child been a child of mine, and had he even *looked* his villainy at my child, I would have brained him as a mad dog, and taken the consequences." The Court and counsel kept up the cross-fire many minutes, till counsel declared that he would stand and argue if it took all summer, and the Court said, "So long as you argue on self-defence, proceed" "You see, gentlemen, how I have been narrowed; but I submit to it, for he is the schoolmaster of the Court." (Laughter)

You see how they have shut out the facts, but yet, like daylight through the blinds, they come in at every crevice. They say, "Don't go into this family quarrel part, of this dangerous assault," and yet their second witness tells you that while Beamer had Baker under and pounded him with a loaded cane he kept on repeating the words between the blows "He has stolen my wife!" "He has *broken up my home!*" "He has destroyed my business!" "He has ruined my family!" "*He has made a prostitute of my wife!*" What else could he do to deserve punishment? Let me illustrate When the gentlemanly burglar called on Oren Scotten at Springwells the other night, the family were fast asleep. It was two o'clock in the morning. The cold steel of a revolver was pressed to

Scotten's temple, and he looked up in the face of a masked man with a dark lantern in one hand and said, "I suppose you want something?" "Yes, get up," said the burglar. He got up. "Fold your hands." He folded his arms meekly. "Show me your money, and no harm will come to you." He hesitated. "Show it!" demanded the burglar He showed it, and when all was taken, $700—a bright diamond ring was seen on the wife's finger. "Take it off," demanded the burglar. The wedding ring was taken off by the husband, who went down and showed the gentleman to the door, and remained so under his control that he bade him call again!

Out in the night went the burglar, back to his home went Scotten. His home was not broken up! His wife and child, his family, were safe, only a little after all was gone! And yet, could he have shot the intruder half-way into the house or half-way out of it, or even if he had met him on the commons and shot him an hour later, the law would justify and excuse the killing. And who will compare the injury of Scotten to the wrongs of Beamer? A home in ruins to a few hundred dollars! Who would not say "Amen" to the killing of a felon?—and yet here is the felon of felons, the greatest felon of the age, a destroyer of homes, who would go unpunished.

Away off in Idaho, where my friend McCulloch, the district attorney, is from—away out beyond the mountains and lava-beds of the far West, they know how to treat hard characters, and when a man becomes too desperate, or when the horse-thieves become too common, they hang up a few to dry in the forests and leave them as a warning to offenders.

Laws are better for it, society is safer; homes are safer, and men sleep easier and more contentedly.

And yet I have hardly reached more than a preface to my argument. Our defence is self-defence. We believe with Blackstone that the law respects human passions. That it becomes lawful sometimes for an injured man to do himself that immediate justice that the case demands, and that he is to be judged by the circumstances as they appeared to him. Laws are NOT strong enough to prevent it—they never will be—never can be strong enough. And in this case what are the circumstances? A once happy home in ruins; a business broken up, a wife stolen from her husband, an armed adversary, face to face with one whom he had ruined. There they are like two armies in battle. There they are in open daylight. To Beamer he was an enemy. To Beamer he was an armed adversary. To Beamer he had committed a crime worse than murder (" he made a prostitute of my wife"). To Beamer he was a dangerous enemy, and as he faced him in the sunlight he saw the fiend who had come into his family And what did Baker do? Picked up a brick. (The Court "He put his hand on his hip pocket first " I THANK your Honour! (Sensation.) Yes, gentlemen, put his hand on his pocket as if reaching for a revolver! Beamer said, "Throw it, you coward!" Baker threw it. They advanced each with a raised cane. Baker struck at Beamer; the blow reached his right wrist in being warded off. It broke Baker's cane in two pieces. No doubt of that —Bridge saw a broken cane. Baker says he burned it in a stove. It must have been broken to be so

burned Beamer strikes Baker over the head a half-
dozen blows, repeating his injuries in the ears of
his enemy. "He has ruined my business. He has
stolen my wife and broken up my home." And they
are separated by force, and Baker goes home for
six weeks to a sick bed, and Beamer goes to gaol
with a lame hand; and I ask you, gentlemen, in
the clear light of these facts, *has not Baker brought
it on himself?*" Did he not deserve all he got?
Would you have done less? Might you not have
done more? You are married men; so am I married,
and well married; my house is my idol, so is yours;
and had Beamer consulted me and told me of his
treatment, of his finding this man in his bedroom, I
would have said, "Go and load both barrels of a
shot-gun, fire one barrel into his body, if it don't
finish him, then another, and see that you aim at his
body while he is in the act, and don't plead insanity,
but say, 'I intended to do it, to avenge the awful
wrong.'" And as heaven is my judge, had one-tenth
of this injury been done to me and my home I would
have followed such a course, and I would not have
pleaded any insanity but self-defence, for laws are not
made to punish such offences adequately in any other
way Stolen his wife, broken up his business, ruined
his home! Think of it. And the villain settled in the
same city, threatening to Beamer's brother that he
would shoot any man who even censured him for it.
Has it come to this? Must homes be so ruined while
honest men, who live up to the ripe old age of fifty-six
years in peace, in order, in industry, and never break
a law, shall be hurried off to prison and the real guilty
ones go free? Away with such laws. It is not

reason, it is not sense, it is not humane, it is not as you would be judged.

The time will come too soon when we shall stand for judgment. The books will be opened. (We shall know each other then.) The mists and clouds will be all torn away and we will be judged by One who sees the motives of us all. The books will be opened and you will be asked, "Have you remembered mercy?" If not, then with what judgment you judge you shall be judged, and they that judge without mercy shall be judged without mercy.

Take this defendant, hand him over if you will to a felon's doom, to a prison ten years—no half-way verdict—either Guilty or Not guilty. Let him end his life in honour or dishonour. It will not be long, gentlemen. If you convict him, go and tell it to your wives, tell over the causes and the result; tell it to the community, tell it to the Press and the world, and let your portraits adorn the illustrated papers as the first jury in two hundred years that has punished the injured one in a case of self-defence. But that you will not do. You cannot find it in your hearts to convict him. It is not in the evidence. He is not guilty He has acted all too slow, but yet in self-defence.

Jury acquitted Beamer in fifteen minutes—that time was spent in wondering why he did not punish the intruder sooner.

LINCOLN'S FIRST MURDER CASE.

THE simplest story of a murder trial is always of interest, and especially so where the case is conducted, on either side, by men with the ability and genius that Abraham Lincoln possessed.

In the July *Century* appears the end of a story of a long case, and includes what is vaguely known as Lincoln's first defence in a murder trial   The details need not be repeated. The pith of the story is instructive to lawyers.

Grayson was charged with shooting Lockwood at a camp meeting, on the evening of August 9, 18—, and with running away from the scene of the killing, which was witnessed by Sovine. The proof was so strong that, even with an excellent previous character, Grayson came very near being lynched on two occasions soon after his indictment for murder.

The mother of the accused, after failing to secure older counsel, finally engaged young Abraham Lincoln, as he was then called, and the trial came on to an early hearing. No objection was made to the jury, and there was no cross-examination of witnesses, save the last and only important one, who swore that he knew the parties, saw the shot fired by Grayson, saw him run away, and picked up the deceased, who died instantly.

The evidence of guilt and identity was morally certain. The attendance was large, the interest intense. Grayson's mother began to wonder why "Abraham remained silent so long and why he didn't *do something*!" The people finally rested. The tall lawyer (Lincoln) stood up and eyed the strong witness in

silence, without books or notes, and slowly began his
defence by these questions:

"And you were with Lockwood just before and
saw the shooting?"

"Yes."

"And stood very near to them?"

"No, about twenty feet away."

"May it not have been *ten* feet?"

"No, it was twenty feet or *more*."

"In the open field?"

"No, in the timber."

"What kind of timber?"

"Beech timber."

"Leaves on it are rather thick in August?"

"Rather."

"And you think *this* pistol was the one used?"

"It looks like it."

"You could see defendant shoot—see how the
barrel hung, and all about it!"

"Yes."

"How near was this to the meeting-place?"

"Three-quarters of a mile away?"

"Where were the lights?"

"Up by the minister's stand."

"Three-quarters of a mile away?"

"Yes; I answered ye *twiste*."

"Did you not see a candle there, with Lockwood or
Grayson?"

"No; what would we want a candle for?"

"How, then, did you see the shooting?"

"By moonlight!" (defiantly).

"You saw this shooting at ten at night—in beech
timber, three-quarters of a mile from the lights; saw

the pistol barrel; saw the man fire; saw it twenty feet away—saw it all by moonlight?   Saw it nearly a mile from the camp lights?"

"Yes, I told you so before."

The interest was now so intense that men leaned forward to catch the smallest syllable.   Then the lawyer drew out a blue-covered almanack from his side coat pocket; opened it slowly, offered it in evidence; showed it to the jury and the Court, read from a page with careful deliberation that the moon on that night was unseen, and only rose at *one* the next morning!

Following this climax Mr Lincoln moved the arrest of the perjured witness as the real murderer, saying, "Nothing but a *motive to clear himself* could have induced him to swear away so falsely the life of one who never did him harm!"   With such determined emphasis did Lincoln present his showing, that the Court ordered Sovine arrested, and under the strain of excitement he broke down and confessed to being the one who fired the fatal shot himself, but denied it was intentional.

This lesson to lawyers, who may not read the whole story, is a good law lecture.   It may be added that Lincoln first determined his client was not guilty; and having settled that point, he knew the story was one made up for a purpose, and that purpose he was bound to discover, and did discover in his own original manner.

As a reader of trials for years, this one presents as keen interest and displays as much sagacity of counsel as any I have found—even Choate or Webster could have done no better; many other trials are more elaborate in detail, many contain passages of wit and arguments of rare eloquence—they are lessons from life and full of wisdom—some of masterful logic, yet none are so great or were so ably conducted as to overshadow this simple victory by a young country lawyer, who lived to be the leader of a nation and filled with honour the highest station in the world.

NERVE IN LAW.

IF every lawyer should express his honest opinion on the one thing lacking in the profession he would answer, "Nerve." It will meet him at the office with his ever-ready client who wants a lawsuit and may not have a case, or the defaulter who would skip out and defraud his creditors of their just claim, or one about to let go his rights rather than contest them in Court or office; in suits or settlements in the business of law, whether trials or counsel, *nerve* is the fine art needed. Within the year an able advocate has won a will-contest reaching into millions, and just as he was about to pick the fruits of his long and earnest effort he was set upon by a couple of blackmailers, and, had he been less nervy than he was, would have been forced to release a large share of his profits, when his nerve stood by him and he became victorious. In another city a transaction reaching nearly a quarter-million was let go by the unnerving of counsel at a point when the contracts were almost completed, and many thousands of earnest-money were deposited. What a test of nerve power was this! As if one seeing a fractious horse tied to a post and frightened by a band should untie the animal and let him run away, rather than hold him to the post till the band

12

passed by. We have all seen these cases during the year—seen angry clients throwing away costs for spite, and others throwing away rights that a little more nerve and coolness would have saved. In this is a wise counsel of greatest value. To-day it is a cattle contract, to-morrow a stock company, next week a business block, later on a street-railway project, or a farm to cut up into city lots, or an option in real estate, or criminal to defend, or a damage suit to settle, nerve is the mettle that a lawyer most should cultivate. As business men are supposed to grow in trade by experience and learn by practice, so age adds new wisdom to the oldest counsel. His books have left out the case that last came to him. Lives, trades, and dealings and conditions are changing. He needs new knowledge If he halts, the busy procession will file past his office door to another counsel as if they saw the signal written, "Behind the times" The competition is so intense in law to-day, the attorneys are so very numerous and their work so exacting, that the fittest and strongest alone succeed To make a bargain about it, and stand by it, requires both nerve and courage.

A MODEST LAWYER.

THERE is a lesson in the life of Geo. F. Edmunds, now deservedly the leading lawyer before the United States Supreme Court, that should interest all members of the profession. Mr. Edmunds is in the prime of life (near sixty), of medium size, rather slim in build, a plain grey-haired man with a mind at once acute, deep, and penetrating, and a logic incomparable A native of Richmond, but a resident of Burlington, Vermont, he has reached an exalted position in his profession   He began life as a poor farmer boy, was educated in the common schools with one half-year's course in an academy at Albany, entered the law office of A B. Maynard at an early age, and later completed his studies with Phelps & Smally, was admitted to practice at twenty-one and early earned distinction in the argument of a Supreme Court case, small in amount, but important in principle   He appeared before the Supreme Court in a homespun suit, with trousers much too short for him, and yet with a skill that attracted the attention of Judge Redfield, who sent for the young man and complimented the effort   He was twice elected to the Legislature and served as Speaker of the House.   He then practised law four years with success and was elected to the State Senate, and from there appointed to fill the vacancy caused by the death of United States Senator Foote.   To the last position he has been re-elected ever since without opposition   Besides being a senator, he has a large and lucrative law practice.   His methods are peculiar.   With a terse, clear brief, and few cases cited, he argues orally, beginning with conceded propositions and reaching logical ends   His views were adopted in the great Maine election case, in which he said in effect that where the Constitution contemplated that a voter had a right to cast a ballot for his choice, if a mere mistake occurred in initials of a name, which could not be a mistake of the person, surely the voter should not be defrauded of his rights by an error of the printer.   His arguments are largely oral; his citations few and well selected; his conclusions irresistible.   Not many months ago he was retained by the House of Lords in

England and called before that august body to expound a principle of American law on heirship. His views were brief and pointed and convincing. The Lords adopted his theory and tendered him a handsome reception, which he modestly declined, and proceeded at once on his journey. Law is natural to him. He is a *born* lawyer. His practice is high-priced, and not less than $1,000 retainers, with a wide range to charge for time and extent of victory. The lesson of his life to lawyers is this. That one need not start high to reach high; that genius with opportunity may command success, that clearness and brevity are taking in argument; that modesty has promoted Edmunds from the farm-boy lawyer through the Legislature to the high rank of a superior counsel of the greatest Court in the world. His whole life has been in a law school, the school of actual experience.

THE TEACHER'S DEFENCE.

It is a country school-teacher's trial for murder. The Court-room is packed to witness a trial that always excites a community. It comes into their homes and interests everyone. The facts are best developed in the argument. The time is December, 1887. The place is Corunna. One hundred scholars are witnesses. The case is strongly represented for the people, who are determined to convict (they have convicted the defendant in their hearts already). Notice the answer of the very first juror sworn, to the question, "Have you formed or expressed an opinion in this case?" "Yes, sir, I have—I have said *I am opposed to the use of firearms in our public schools.*"

(Sensation.) This reflects the average bias. A jury is obtained and a separation of witnesses ordered—one brought in at a time. Before any evidence is given, both the people and defendant's counsel carefully state their case.

The people opened their case by reading the charge, that the defendant did, on December 8, 1886, at Henderson, wilfully, intentionally, and feloniously kill Thomas Morrison, &c., and promised to show that Joscelyn had told the children, who wished to do so, to go out at recess, as he was about to punish Calvin Morrison, a thirteen-year-old son of deceased. He pictured the whipping, the shooting, the vast array of children to prove it, the pain and agony of Morrison, the kneeling wife at his side, fanning him till his death, and closed by saying he presumed the broken words of deceased in his agony would be used to excuse defendant.

The proof was strong on both sides. A single incident reveals a discrepancy. A scholar who saw the shooting swore that the teacher walked to his desk, took out his revolver, put it in his coat-pocket on the front right-hand side, from which he drew it when he fired at Morrison This looked premeditated. On cross-examination it appeared defendant *had no such pocket in the coat worn on that occasion.*

Every available inch of space in the Court-room was occupied, every window filled with faces of those who stood twenty deep at each possible point of hearing, while beyond surged crowds of those unable to hear, but impatiently awaiting the result. Indeed, before the defendant's counsel had half finished his introductory address, whispers were heard on every

side, " He's going to win the case." It was certainly
one of the most intensely interesting and dramatic trials
that have taken place in many years.

The defence said : We are assembled, gentlemen, to
investigate an accident that caused a human life to go
out under circumstances that excite our interest and
compel our attention. It appeared early to you that
my friend told you but a portion of this strange story
Let me tell more of it, as proven in evidence. Alfred
Joscelyn, the defendant, is twenty-nine years old,
born in New York State, educated, refined, of industrious habits, never before accused of any offence—
indeed of such a mild and quiet disposition that he
couldn't, if he would, wilfully injure anyone. He was
a sash and door maker, and worked at his father's
trade until a year and a half ago, when his left thumb
was torn off in a machine, and he became a cripple in
that hand. The effect was a serious shock to his
system. He grew sleepless, nervous, lost flesh, and
suffered from blood-poisoning. The wound was a
half-year in healing, and when he was able to do
light work he engaged to teach the village school at
Henderson, where he taught two terms.

Owing to some jealousy on account of his brother
being a director, who helped hire him, but mainly
because of its being a hard district, trouble commenced early in the fall of '86, and the children took
sides against the teacher.

It is morning and at recess. Calvin Morrison, an
unruly boy, is about to be punished. He was a
fighter, and could swear in all the modern oaths of
the season. He would run away, and tell the teacher
he would be d——d if he would come in. The big

boys laughed.   It was very funny to them.   He
called the boy to punish him   The boy fought back,
and was conquered.   In the tussle a whip was broken
over the boy's arm   Another was snatched from the
teacher's hand by the boy, and recoiled on his nose,
and it bled.   The boy rubbed the blood over one side
of his face and smeared it.   School was called again,
and suddenly in came Morrison, the boy's father, a
large man of one hundred and ninety pounds;
Joscelyn weighed one hundred and twenty-two.   One
was a slender cripple, one, a giant in strength!
Morrison was angry.   Throwing his hat on the desk,
he muttered:

"I want to know what in hell you're whipping my
boy for!" starting toward the teacher, who said, "For
disobeying the rules and running away."

"Didn't you lick him for that yesterday?"

"No!"

"Well, if you ever lay your hand on him again,
damn you! I'll pound you into the ground!"

He turns to go.   He sees his boy's face   He turns
to Joscelyn and says, "*Damn* you, I've a notion to
do it now!"

He rushes to the desk.   Joscelyn draws his
revolver from his hip-pocket and says· "Hold on,
Mr. Morrison!   You lay yourself liable for disturbing
a school."

On rushes Morrison to the rostrum   He clinches
the teacher with his right hand thrown over his neck,
and reaches with his left hand for the revolver now
held off to the right at arm's length.   The struggle is
desperate.   In the extreme moment of excitement and
peril, Nature or instinct prompts the thought to

Joscelyn, "O God! Must I shoot? *Must I kill him!*"
The light goes out in his eyes. The room whirls.
He loses his control. He knows not what has happened—whether an accident or a pull at the hammer
has let go the dangerous bullet! Morrison is hit in
the abdomen. The ball passes through the left lapel
of Joscelyn's coat, it is buried in Morrison's bowels;
but the strong man struggles, swearing, "Let go of
it! Let go of it!" In a moment he wilts and
weakens, and mutters· "There! I can't hurt you
now! You've shot me!" still lying on the teacher.

Joscelyn says, "Get up, and maybe I can help
you."

He cannot get up. The small man rolls the large
one off, examines the wound; sees the pale deathly
look, sends for a doctor—none can be found, goes
for a team, hurries to Owosso, sends a doctor, gives
himself up, is bailed, is here on trial for something
you, or *you*, would have done in his place—for
something he could not *help* doing, for something
Morrison brought upon himself, for something that
laws cannot control, for the law of Nature prompts it
in all men and all animals. It is inbred and inborn.
The law of ages sanctions it. Our own State
sanctions it, and by three separate decisions has said:
"The man when hard pressed by one of superior
strength and violent temper is to act under the circumstances *as they appear to him.* He is not obliged
to even call upon bystanders for help, but may defend
himself even to the taking of life, and it will be excusable homicide. He may or may not be in actual
serious danger, but if he *believes* that he is, he may
act, and he is not expected to draw any very fine dis-

tinctions when he believes his life is in peril, or his body is in danger of serious harm "

Such is the law of our State beyond all question; and such is the law of reason, of instinct, and Nature.

But we have it in evidence. We have shown you his father, who knew of this terrible accident by the machine, of his peculiar dread and fear of danger, we called his brother and proved the warning to the young man as to Morrison's quarrelsome disposition— a man who was hard to handle—who had five fights a year on an average   We called in the neighbours who have seen him break in the head of a sugar-barrel with his fist, who have seen him kick an old man till he was senseless, who knew him to be violent and dangerous,—to deny this powerful army of trained scholars, who ran away confused and excited, who claim the teacher fired twice; who heard the breaking desk as it was wrenched from the floor, who saw no smoke, who found a hole an inch square in the plaster, but no bullet, who admit the anger, the swearing, and the clinching, but saw no need of using a revolver.

In his schoolroom Joscelyn was in his home! Who but he should guard and control it? Who but he should ward off invaders? Who but he should enforce order? His home was invaded, and he acted under the law of self-defence, that in our State makes him the judge of his own danger and permits him when so assaulted to repel the assault, even to the taking of life, and defines such an act as excusable homicide.

It is clear, then, by the evidence of both sides, that there was an occasion for self-defence, which Cicero says is " A law that we are not trained in, but

which is implanted in us; that if our life is in danger
by robbers or enemies, every means of securing safety
is honourable. . . . Reason has taught this law to
learned men; necessity, to barbarians; custom, to all
nations, and Nature, to wild beasts."

Besides this, gentlemen, I assert that laws are not
strong enough, statutes are not broad enough, and
never can be created by man, to restrain his own arm
from warding off danger when his life is in peril! As
it *appeared to him*, you are to judge him! He was
almost alone at recess The boys were out He
was set upon and frightened. He must act, and act
instantly. He must contend with a giant—with an
intruder without warning.

He had been enforcing the lesson that the way to
stop crime is to *stop raising criminals!*

And think of the lesson you would teach, if you
convicted him for standing at his post in a time of
danger! You would strike a blow at our common-
school system that is a centre column of our
civilisation.

* * * * *

I have said, gentlemen, that bad boys make bad
men. Let me illustrate At a reunion in the old
schoolhouse where I was trained as a boy, my first
teacher, Albert Kenyon, spoke like this

" For nine years I taught this Union school—often
with few books and many scholars in an early day—
always with young men and women older and larger
than myself. Many were punished, for it was more
the custom then than now. Often have I been
threatened secretly that they would ' get even with the
teacher some day '—(meaning when big enough, I sup-

pose)—but no one ever struck back. Scholars, I have watched the progress of these boys and girls as they grew to manhood and to womanhood, many have outgrown their teacher in size and ability to master him. I have seen the studious children of the poor— little boys with patches on their trousers, and little girls with blue dress of calico—grow up to men and women, and far outstrip, and stand head and shoulders over their more favoured fellows in eminence; and I have concluded that good boys make good men, and good girls make good women. And I tell you with pain and with pride that one—only one—of my scholars turned out badly, he was unruly, ran away, went to the bad, and ended in prison—brought his father's grey hairs with sorrow to the grave."

Ah, gentlemen, what a story this is, and how true after all! Have we not learned it by bitter experience that bad boys make bad men? And do we not know that good boys make good men?

Look about you! Look at this Court-house and see this array of Henderson boys and girls, urged on by their parents to fight a school-teacher—urged on to sustain this Calvin Morrison, a boy of only thirteen summers, whose curly brow wears the scowl of crime, who swears and damns his teacher, and fights back and brings his own father to the grave! Great Heavens! has it come to this! Has the sense of decency sunk so low that a community can take such sides and set such an atrocious example? (Great sensation in the Court room.) "And the king walked out and bared his head weeping, saying, O Absalom, my son, Absalom, my son! O, my son, would God had I died for thee! Absalom, my son, my son!"

I must leave you, never to speak to you perhaps till we shall all stand for judgment. We will know each other then, our masks will all be torn away. I ask you to deal fairly, humanely, mercifully with this young man! I ask you to uphold the cause that *he* upheld! I ask you to set an example to dangerous men and check *the raising of bad boys in our country!*

To him, imprisonment would be more than death. Death in honour, at any age, is not to be so much dreaded as a life of dishonour. "Whether a wall or a door, death undoubtedly opens into a better life. The heavens are full of worlds, by the side of which ours is a speck." But to walk up and down a narrow cell for years; to come out at last, if at all, broken in body and mind, and say, as the man did after six years of prison life at Auburn, "How sweet the air smells outside to-day! I never knew the sunshine was so good before!"

But it *will* not happen! It *cannot* happen!

The last words of Morrison told, as he went to meet his God, are said to you. It is the death scene. I call him from the clouds to tell you now. Here is Morrison—the dying man—in the presence of two ministers and his family, aware of his approaching death, after he had twice been prayed with, asking

"Where is Joscelyn!"

"He has gone for the doctor, to Owosso."

"What!—gone for a doctor for me?"

"Yes."

"Is there no hope for me?"

"Not in this world," said the minister.

"Then tell Joscelyn I ask his forgiveness. He will forgive me. I had no business there!" And next to the name of the Saviour, the name of Joscelyn and his forgiveness was the last thought of the dying man Morrison

Shall we say any more, gentlemen? "Where is Joscelyn? I want to ask his forgiveness. I had no business there!"—going to his home beyond the stars, muttering the self-condemning words, in effect, "He is innocent!"

He *is* innocent! May God help you to give him a quick deliverance!

*   *   *   *   *

The jury said, "Not guilty!"

CONCLUSION.

1. Look at the profit side of the ledger, money is handy in law business.

2. Rely on a personal study of cases; a few, well sorted, are better than many of remote bearing.

3. Bring fewer suits and settle more, even by splitting differences, but *charge for it.*

4. Counsel less with clients and more with witnesses. the bias of the one overreaches; the timidity of the other falls short of truth.

5. Cross-examine less with honest witnesses; they tell too much and misplace it so recklessly.

6. Claim not too much perfection in clients; the jury know human nature is ugly; they will be jealous of *half-angels* in lawsuits.

7. Demand less and be believed, rather than claim too much and let the jury halve it, they may give the big half to your adversary.

8. Use others as you hope to be used by them; the chances of gain and loss are in favour of the gain side by this method, and a good name will be a fortune made easy.

9. Carry your heart into Court—in everything, do nothing heedlessly; juries are more and more in sympathy with fair play every year, and no theory will stand testing like honesty.

10. Don't forget the boy lawyers, struggling up the steep hill from college to Webster's top storey It's a long way up now. It is better to cheer than to discourage. Cheer them, and they will brighten your name hereafter.

Lightning Source UK Ltd.
Milton Keynes UK
UKOW05n1325071016

284730UK00001B/38/P